Julian Hawthorne

The Spectre of the Camera

A Romance

Julian Hawthorne

The Spectre of the Camera
A Romance

ISBN/EAN: 9783744696142

Printed in Europe, USA, Canada, Australia, Japan

Cover: Foto ©Thomas Meinert / pixelio.de

More available books at **www.hansebooks.com**

THE

SPECTRE OF THE CAMERA

OR

The Professor's Sister

A ROMANCE

BY

JULIAN HAWTHORNE

AUTHOR OF

'A DREAM AND A FORGETTING' 'DAVID POINDEXTER'S DISAPPEARANCE'
'DUST' ETC.

London
CHATTO & WINDUS, PICCADILLY
1888

CONTENTS.

THE

SPECTRE OF THE CAMERA.

CHAPTER I.

METAPHYSICS.

'WHAT is memory, I should like to know?'
said Will Burlace, using the end of his broad
middle finger as a tobacco-stopper. 'How
does it work, Ralph, my boy? Do we remember everything in our experience, as some
philosophers hold, or does each of us take out
of the past only that which belongs to his
character and temperament, or are recollection
and oblivion a mere lottery, over which we
have no control, or——'

And what is the exact difference between

B

memory and imagination ?' I broke in. 'We say the past has no existence : neither have the conceptions of the imagination. And I have heard of people imagining things until they believed them true.'

'Yes, why not ?' added Burlace, with a grin. 'We are taught that the external world itself is but a prejudice of the mind. There is no reality but thought and will. Our present is a dream ; our past and future are the ghosts of dreams. You cannot make out imagination to be anything less than that. We talk about the creations of poets and novelists, and it is notorious that many of the personages of fiction from Homer to Balzac, live with a vitality that would put to shame Methuselah, or Augustus the Strong. Where shall we draw the line?'

'The senses originate in the brain,' continued I : 'don't they end there as well ? we may admit that we feel sensations, but how do we know that the feeling and the thing felt are not two visions of the same thing?'

'Look at ghosts, spectres, and the supernatural generally,' said Burlace, blowing a cloud of smoke into fantastic shapes and waving his big hand through them. 'What is the difference between a ghost and an ordinary human being?'

'As a general rule,' said Ralph, who had been sitting meanwhile on his back and shoulders, with his slippered feet broad against the tall porcelain stove which, as everywhere in Germany, dominated the apartment, 'as a general rule, the difference between a ghost and an ordinary human being is this:—only one person sees the ghost, whereas the ordinary human being has been, is, or can be seen by whomsoever chooses to look at him. And a similar distinction might be drawn as between the contents of the memory and those of the imagination. If I tell you an incident of my past life, and you don't believe it, I can adduce living witnesses in support of my statement: but if I tell you a story, or a lie, and you are incredulous, I can only keep on lying.'

'I would confess and repent, if I were you,' interposed Burlace.

'What is that theory of yours about apparitions?' I inquired.

'Oh, it would take me too far back to explain that,' answered Ralph lazily.

'It's one the professor told him, and he's forgotten it,' Burlace asserted, winking at me across the table.

'The professor is a Buddhist,' said Ralph. 'For my part, I believe neither in re-incarnation, Karma, Devachan, Nirvana, nor the Astral light.'

Burlace grinned again. 'Nor in anything else!'

' Yes,' returned Ralph, in the same lazy tone, ' I believe in God, in the Divine inspiration of the Bible, in the Incarnation, in the immortality of the soul, and in the possible intercourse between the dead and the living, among other things.'

' A nice creed for the prize student of a German university ! But I suppose you are lying, now.'

' I am casting my pearls before Burlace, which is perhaps as bad.'

' Well, to begin with, what is matter?'

' Matter is the attestation of the constancy of the relation between the Creator and the creature.'

' Oh ! and what is nature ? '

' Nature is the analysis of human nature, projected on the sphere of sense by the creative energy.'

' If that be the case,' said I, ' why does not the face of nature become modified in correspondence with our growth and develop·ment ?'

' Well,' returned Ralph, ' doesn't it ?'

' I haven't noticed it in my own experience,' I replied.

' You would, if you were mankind. And even you furnish your room and dig your garden in accordance with your notion of the correct thing. But the great geological and cosmical changes, the variation and extinction of species, alterations of climate, and all matters of that calibre, follow and reflect the development of Humanity with a big H. And, by the way, that's the basis of what you call my theory of apparitions.'

' How so ?'

' Oh, don't encourage him ! ' cried Burlace.

' You have the visible object on one side,' Ralph said, ' and the brain on the other. The eye is the connecting link. The light reflected from objects reaches the brain through the eye,

and the brain thereupon translates it into ideas
of things. Such is the accepted doctrine.
But in certain moods of abstraction and concentration you are hardly conscious of the
external world, and the images of the mind
assume a corresponding substantiality. If
now a disembodied being applies itself strongly
to your own spirit, your spiritual organ of
sight—which is the eye within the eye—perceives it as a—what Burlace calls—ordinary
human being.'

'Oh, my wig!' muttered Burlace.

'But how does your ontological theory—'

'Why, it's simple enough. We perceive
an ordinary human being by virtue of that
universal human constitution that we share
with the race ; but we perceive an apparition
by virtue of a special and finite impression
wrought upon us by an unembodied spirit.
The action of the organ of vision is the same
in the one case as in the other : the appari-

tion is, to the person seeing it, as real as an actual man.   Yet it is not real, but an illusion, because it is an individual, and not a general experience.'

'But an apparition is a spirit; do you call a spirit an illusion ? '

'An apparition is not a spirit.'

'Neither, certainly, is it a physical being.'

'No ; it is the reflection upon the sphere of sense of a being who is not physical.   It is an illusion in the same way that your reflection in the looking-glass is an illusion— it is nothing in itself, but a reality causes it.'

'May I be permitted to offer one suggestion in the premises ? ' inquired Burlace.

'No,' said Ralph.

'Well, here it is.   Sense, according to you, only seems to convey messages from without ; in truth it is concerned solely with what proceeds from within,—for the obvious reason that the entire material universe is but the phenomenal externisation of the elements of the human mind—have I got the lingo right ?'

'Viewing the universe, of course, from the point of view of use, not of form and extension,' supplemented Ralph, closing his eyes.

'Just as you please about that ! well, now, your apparition is visible to the eye—or to the eye within the eye, if you like that better—say, to the sense of vision. But it is generally admitted that all our senses are but modifications of one sense, to wit, the sense of touch. Are you listening ?'

'No ; because I knew from the start what you were driving at.'

'Oh, indeed! and pray what was it ?'

'That an apparition that can be seen, ought, by logical inference, to be also an object of touch, hearing, smell, and taste.'

'Well, and how are you going to wriggle

out of that dilemma ?' demanded Burlace, with a snort.

'I am comfortable where I am. I don't perceive your dilemma. I hold your inference to be unimpeachable.'

'Do you mean to say that a ghost can be handled—'

'Heard, smelt, and tasted. Certainly, why not ?'

'And yet you call it an illusion!'

'But with a reality behind it!'

'I am going home,' said Burlace, getting up from his chair with a grotesque assumption of decrepitude. 'I am a very foolish, fond old man. I don't catch on any longer. I have been getting things wrong end foremost all these years. Matter, it seems, is but the attestation of the constancy of a relation,— therefore I ought to be able to walk through a block of houses, or pass my arm through a girl's waist instead of round it. Apparitions, on the contrary, can be felt and smelt as well as seen, therefore I presume that I have been consorting hitherto with apparitions. In fact, what am I myself but an apparition—an illusion with a reality behind me ? I have heard of people being made nervous by having a spectre behind them ; but fancy the condition of a poor spectre with a reality behind him ! Let me get away, while reason yet holds her seat in this distracted globe ! '

' And all because I happened to remark that memory is what is meant by the creation of man male and female,' said Ralph, with a sigh.

' Imbecility, thy name is metaphysics ! ' muttered Burlace, as he opened the door and closed it behind him with a bang. So Ralph Merlin and I were left alone in front of the tall porcelain stove.

Those delightful old student days in Dresden, twenty years ago ! What good times we had !—not because of what we did, but because we so enjoyed doing it. What did we do, in fact ? we drank beer out of glass schoppen with porcelain covers ; we smoked pipes and Laferme cigarettes ; we attended open-air concerts in the Grosser Garten, the Bruehlsche Terrace, the Waldschlösschen ; we fought schläger duels, and wore high boots, black velveteen jackets, and caps four inches in diameter ; we went to masked balls, where neither we nor anybody else behaved quite properly ; we went to other dances in queer places ; we thought we owned the earth and the fulness thereof; and we talked metaphysics. There is nothing to compare with the zeal with which young men of a certain age and intellectual training will talk metaphysics. They know all that Hegel, Kant, Schopenhauer and Spinoza knew, and demonstrate that these gentlemen did not go nearly far, nor half deep enough, and were much too

lucid and straightforward in all their state-
ments. We began where they left off, and
stopped nowhere. We dissolved the Universe and created it again each after a recipe
of his own. As to society—civilisation—I
shudder to think how we objurgated and
annihilated them. And morality ! Burlace
had a thermometer in his room, which he
used to call The Register of Virtue. It was
a huge affair, about five feet long, and I
believe he had stolen it from the outside of a
druggist's shop. Opposite each space of ten
degrees he had pasted the photograph of a
woman. Between the 30th and 40th degrees
she was muffled up from her chin to her toes,
and wore a big hood. Between the 40th and
50th her hood was off and her pelisse was un-
buttoned. Between the 50th and 60th the
pelisse had disappeared and you could discern
the outlines of her figure. The 70th degree
limit showed her in full ball costume, very dé-

colletée.   At the 80th her costume had shrunk at both ends, and she was now a ballet dancer, very much on one leg.   The next interval was difficult to describe ; and the final one revealed Eve pure and simple.   When, therefore, the conversation turned upon moral questions, Burlace would point to this new Jacob's Ladder and say : ' The whole problem is settled there, gentlemen.   I make no comments ; none are needed.   Let each man of you select the latitude that suits him best, and be happy.   The equator is good enough for me.'

Burlace was able, obstinate, boisterous ; a scoffer and a sceptic.   He had a broad sense of humour, but was apt to become oppressive. His great, strident voice ate up all other sounds, and finally made one's ears indignant. But he would stand by you in trouble, and, after bullying you to your face, take your part behind your back.   He and Ralph

Merlin and I were, at that time, the only
Americans there; so we were a good deal
together. Ralph and Burlace were generally
chaffing each other: I used to take part,
sometimes against one, sometimes against the
other. But, at bottom, Ralph was my friend.
I was often in doubt whether to take him
seriously or in jest, but I had an instinct of
affection towards him. And I understood
better than any of his other companions the
moods of his mind and heart.

CHAPTER II.

RALPH AND HIS QUEER NOTIONS.

RALPH MERLIN was, I believe, of Philadelphia extraction. His family had been wealthy for several generations, and that, in America, means culture and high breeding. Ralph was of a fine patrician type. His physical organisation was delicate as a watch spring, but strong, healthy, and unweariable. He and Burlace (who weighed just ninety pounds more than Ralph did) had a wrestling match one day. After a while, Ralph got a grip on Burlace somehow, and began slowly to bend him over backwards. It was the power of one backbone against the other. Burlace, who prided himself on his strength, and was always asking us to feel his muscle, tugged and struggled like a bull. His broad visage became red, his throat swelled, and a great purple vein started out in his forehead. He grinned a hideous grin, showing his big teeth set together. All the while he was being forced over, inch by inch. Ralph's face did not show signs of the tremendous exertion he must have been making ; only his eyes, which were fixed on Burlace's, seemed to grow steadily larger and brighter ; and his slender hands gripped those great, brawny muscles of Burlace's as a steel vice grips green wood. At last, just as Burlace's eyes rolled up, and he was about to gasp and collapse, Ralph suddenly loosed his hold and laughed. Burlace sat down on the floor, panting and perspiring.

' You're too big for me,' said Ralph ; and a thin stream of blood ran down his chin. At first I was startled, thinking he had ruptured a blood-vessel ; but he had only bitten through his lower lip. 'Well,' grunted Will Burlace, as soon as he could speak, 'then I thank my stars I'm no smaller, that's all.'

Ralph had beautiful, arched feet, and there was a just perceptible arch in his nose, too ; thin, wide nostrils, broad, straight eyebrows, black, over gray eyes, black wavy hair, fine white complexion.   His upper lip was slender, the lower full, curving under sharply to a round Roman chin.   I never saw a more thoroughly masculine face ; and his deep bass voice suited it.

He had plenty of brains, and managed them well.   He had graduated at Yale college when he was but eighteen years old ; afterwards he had spent three years at Cambridge in England, and now he was taking an engineering course in Germany.   He might have lived a luxurious club and yacht existence if he had cared to.   But he was not contented with his inherited possessions ; he wanted a profession too. Whether, having got it, he would ever practise it, was another question ; but there was no doubt about his getting it. He was esteemed the best student of his time. Yet he had not been devoting himself exclusively to his nominal pursuit, by any means. He had interested himself for some years past in esoteric philosophy and religion ; and here in Dresden he had met a man who was already very far advanced on the road Ralph was travelling.

This was Professor Conrad Hertrugge. The Professor was then about thirty years old, and by no means a general favourite with his classes. He was as sharp and cold as an ice-chisel, in the class-room. There was a strong sarcastic vein in him, which he was apt to use unmercifully ; and to the common run of people he was so curt and unsympathetic that they found it impossible to get up any conversation with him ; and after one or two attempts, they were glad to give him a wide berth.

He was a pale, meagre man, with reddish hair, a sardonic mouth, and strange green eyes, which sometimes had red sparkles in them. But there was power in his every feature and gesture,—the power of character, knowledge, and purpose. He had also a power of another kind, rarer, and imperfectly understood. Whether the result of organisation, special training, or both, it was certainly an odd and mysterious faculty. There are more names than one for it, but a name is not an explanation. For my part, I have never been sensible of the influence which such persons are undoubtedly able to exercise ; but I have seen Conrad Hertrugge do what I can only describe as taking a man's will and consciousness out of him, and putting his own in its place. They would call it, nowadays, inhibition of the cortical centres of the brain.

There is no objection, that I know of, to that way of accounting for it.

The Professor, on his first meeting with Ralph, seemed to conceive a pronounced aversion to him. But in the course of two or three months, this aversion changed to a very intimate friendship. I never knew exactly what caused the change, but I have always surmised that Ralph had on some occasion, and in some unobtrusive but effective manner, intimated his incredulity of the Professor's occult abilities ; and that he had been led, subsequently, to recant his disbelief. There was no doubt that he would have made his recantation freely and frankly, when he was once convinced ; and it was not in human nature, nor even in Conrad Hertrugge, to resist Ralph Merlin when he wished to make himself agreeable. At all events, as I say, they became close friends, and were a great deal together ; and since both were, with this

exception, inclined to be solitary, their inti-
macy was the more conspicuous. What they
communed about was of course matter of conjecture ; but some of the conjectures were ~~well~~
enough to have got the pair of them burned for
witches two hundred years ago.

For my part, I was an old comrade of
Ralph's, having known him before he went
to England ; and Ralph admitted to me that
he and Conrad were investigating certain obscure subjects together. He remarked, however, that he did not agree with Conrad as to
the general scheme of things, and was inclined to explain certain phenomena on
another basis than his. To other people—
to Will Burlace for example—Ralph took
pleasure in making enigmatical replies, which
might mean anything or nothing, and which
left them in doubt whether he were poking
fun at them, or were out of his head. But
there was another consideration involved

which neither I nor others had yet heard
of.

When Burlace had left us that evening,
Ralph and I sat smoking, one on each side of
the stove, and for a time kept silence.

'Do you know why Burlace keeps coming
here?' inquired Ralph, at length. He asked
the question, not as one seeking information
as to the fact, but in order to discover
whether my idea accorded with his own.

'Well, we are all three Americans, you
know,' I said.

'Yes. But Burlace wants to have a
definite opinion on all subjects. He can't
endure uncertainty, and he is still uncertain
whether I am a knave or a fool. When he
has made up his mind about that, you won't
see him here again.'

'Whether you are a knave or a fool?'

'In other words, whether I really believe
in the mysteries of the soul, or only pretend

to do so for ends of my own. In the former case I am a fool, in the latter, a knave. I made some progress to-night in recommending to him the latter alternative.'

'You imply that he is incapable of believing in the soul himself.'

'Yes ; that is one of the points on which his mind is made up.'

'Why don't you, or the Professor, convert him ?'

'He hasn't the temperament, for one thing. He can be useful in his own place and way; as a mystic, he would be a nuisance to himself and others.'

'What sort of a mystic would I make ?'

'I have asked myself that question, and so has Conrad.'

'Well ?'

'Well, to be an initiate, one must have initiative. You are too lazy. You are appreciative, and quick of apprehension ; you will listen to all that is told you, understand it, and even believe it, if it accords with your view of the reasonable. But you would stop there. You would never take any action upon the information. By and by, it would fade out of your mind. However much you might be a spiritualist in theory, in practice you will always be a materialist; and the older you grow, the more will that be the case.'

'After all, Ralph, is there anything in it? Granting occultism all it claims, will it ever produce any effect in this world? Can you get further than to affect the imagination and the nerves? Supposing you possess the secret of the universe, can you avail yourself of it to benefit or influence practical men? Or do these magical powers (if there be any) afford anything except subjective entertainment to the wielders of them, and curiosity and mystification to outsiders?'

' You have seen something of what Conrad can do.'

' I have seen him put a man to sleep, and then compel him to act out his dreams. But, at most, that will simply enable some men to make cats'-paws of some others. And that has been done, without magic, since the world began.'

' Magic means the production of something out of nothing,' replied Ralph : ' and that, of course, is an absurdity, because *ex nihilo nihil fit*. No man can create anything, because he has nothing of his own to create it out of. He can produce an illusion, and that is all. The illusion is temporary, often momentary ; and as it seems out of reason, the effect on the mind is also transient. The power of reading and imparting thoughts, without the aid of the senses, and of communicating impressions at a distance, is curious and striking ; but the electric telegraph, in the development it will presently receive, will accomplish the same results more certainly and regularly. My belief is that you can allow the adepts all that they claim of control over the forces of Nature, and yet match them, either now or hereafter, with the matter-of-fact resources of science. I have no doubt that science will not only enable us to travel all over this earth, and converse with its inhabitants, while sitting at home in our easy chairs, but to visit planets, and hold intercourse with other varieties of mankind in the same way. But all that, and a great deal more of the same sort, is simply an advanced materialism, in which I am but moderately interested.'

'It is intercourse with spirits that attracts you.'

'Why should it?'

'Do you believe, then, that so-called spiritual communications are merely the effects of unconscious cerebration and telepathy, and of a sort of electric or magnetic force contained in the human body ? '

'Well, I don't know why we should trouble ourselves to invent so many handsome names for a very obvious fact.   If you believe you have a soul—a spirit—the rest follows of course.   Your spirit is in a certain temporary phase or plane, which we call the material. But it is also in the spiritual world, though not consciously so.   And in that world it must necessarily be surrounded by a multitude of spirits most similar in character and genius to itself.   But your spirit, owing to your being in a different plane of being, is as imperceptible to them as they are to you.'

'Do you mean that there can be no intercourse ? '

'There is constant and universal unconscious intercourse.'

'If it be unconscious, how can you assert that it exists ? '

'You may know it by the analogy of ordinary human intercourse on this material plane.'

'How so?'

'Men are only partly conscious of one another here. I see your body and your house, I hear your words and mark your actions. But what do I know of your nature, your thoughts, your emotions? I guess at them, from such data as I have, and such inferences as I have skill to draw. But you and I may go through life within arm's reach of each other, and yet never once penetrate beyond the veil of each other's faces—never know each other, as the phrase is. All that each of us secretly feels to be himself is invisible and often unsuspected by the other. But the part of us (and it is the larger and more important part) that is invisible here, is visible in the spiritual world. There, our thoughts and nature—our mental scenery—

appear as things. All that makes us what
we are is seen there ; only the personal form
that we identify with ourselves is absent—
living in a foreign country. And that spiritual domain of ours is continually visited and
examined by such spirits as are of similar
mould and inclinations with our own. They
are of both good and evil quality, for there is
good and evil in every man ; and according
as we turn ourselves to good or to evil, is the
complexion of our spiritual guests dark or
light.'

This theory, which Ralph stated with unusual gravity and earnestness, struck me as
being rather bold, to say the least of it ; and
yet I could not deny that it seemed in keeping
with what we know of the laws of spiritual
harmony and association. I had never before
heard Ralph talk in this way.

'If there is such a barrier as you suppose
between the material and the physical planes,'

I said, ' and the intercourse is unconscious on both sides, how do you account for the phenomena of spiritualism ? '

' The barrier is broken down from our side,' Ralph answered.

' By what means ? '

' If I want you to know a thought that is in my mind, I make certain audible sounds, or draw certain visible signs, which, by common agreement, shall convey that thought to you. Speech is a symbol, by which we bridge over the gulf between the world of the mind and that of the body. In a similar way —by a system of symbols—we converse with spirits.'

' But spirits cannot hear our voices, nor we theirs.'

' Symbols are queer things,' returned Ralph ; ' and all spells are symbols. If you hear a spoken word, it arouses the corresponding thought in your mind. The things that we do in the flesh produce effects in the spiritual world ; and certain things, done with a certain purpose, draw the spirits that are nearest to us into direct contact with our plane.   They are sensible of an attraction —an invitation—and they comply with it. In so doing, they necessarily colour themselves with our personality, and can use only the contents of our memory, though so combining them as to produce effects of novelty and surprise.   That is the ground of the " unconscious cerebration " theory.   But what is it that causes the brain to cerebrate unconsciously ?   It is not our initiative ; then it must be some other ; and that other can only be the spirit's.'

' If you really believe you can communicate with spirits, I can't understand your not feeling interested in it.'

' The interest is limited to the fact of the communication ; when that has been experi-

enced, there is nothing else to come. No
spirit can tell us anything that we do not
know, or had not the means of knowing,
without him. And the society of such spirits
as can communicate with us is distinctly
detrimental. They are of the lowest and
crudest class ; they have not found their
place in their own world, and are therefore
still lingering about the confines of this,—
like stray dogs round the door of a butcher's
shop. They will say whatever they think
you expect them to say, in order to get into
still closer terrestrial relations, and conse-
quently they will lie indefinitely. On the
other hand, the imagination of ignorant and
superstitious people is excited by the idea of
communion with the other world, and they
conceive all manner of wild and vapid theories,
every one of which is promptly confirmed by
the equally foolish and unprincipled spirits.
Both parties to the dialogue grow worse and

worse as time goes on ; so that it's no
wonder that the affair generally ends, on our
side, with insanity, murder, or suicide.   What
is there to interest a reasonable person in all
that ?'

'But why should not spirits of a higher
order come to us sometimes ?   Are there no
angels to tell us the truths of heaven and
teach us divine wisdom and goodness ?'

'There are angels, no doubt,' said Ralph ;
'but there is no ground for supposing that
they ever come here.   Their state must be so
entirely different from ours that mutual approach would be impossible.   Besides, the
only spiritual instruction that is worth anything, and whose effects are lasting, must
come from our own consciences, and that
means that it comes direct from God, who
created us and the angels too.   No third
person can ever mediate between Him and
any of His creatures.   His aim is not to bully

us by signs and wonders, but to induce us to find our own way, and help ourselves. If you act under constraint, it is not you, but your constrainer, who acts.'

'Then, if there's nothing worth attention in these things,' said I, 'why do you concern yourself about them at all ?'

'On the contrary, I am just beginning to perceive that there is something worth attention—and very much worth it, too ! Though the spirits can tell us nothing about the next world, it is in our power to find out a great deal about it for ourselves. If Conrad were not so confirmed a Buddhist, we might go far together.'

'He doesn't agree with you ?'

'Buddhists are all materialists at bottom ; what they call spirit is but a refined form of matter. His results are sensational, and have a fascination of their own. But I'm afraid they will get him into trouble yet. Life is a great deal simpler, as well as a great deal profounder than he thinks.   He could easily do a great deal of harm ; I doubt if he could do much good.   He has a fancy that he and I are involved together in some way.   I must say I hope he's mistaken.   By the way, you haven't seen his step-mother, have you ? '

'I didn't know he had one.'

'Well, he has, and she's a very handsome young woman.   She can't be over five-and-twenty.   Conrad's father was near seventy when he married her, and died six months ago, after a year of felicity—if felicity it was.'

'Do she and Conrad get on well to-gether ? '

'I don't believe they do.   There is some question of property, I think. Conrad's sister is in the step-mother's way, and—'

'He has a sister, too ? '

'A girl of nineteen or so. I have never seen her—but, by the way, she was to have come home yesterday, and Conrad asked me to come to his house this evening. Let us go and have a look at the young lady—the two young ladies. It is only half-past eight, and we can dress and be there by nine.'

' By all means,' said I. And we went.

CHAPTER III.

TWO WOMEN.

PROFESSOR CONRAD HERTRUGGE occupied a handsome *étage* on a street adjoining the public garden. His father had been a merchant, and had accumulated a great deal of money. But having begun life poor, and never having had time to amuse himself, he had not acquired the habit of luxury, and his house, until the time of his second marriage, had been as bare as a barn,—so Ralph told me. But his new wife had changed all that. She was handsome and ambitious, and demanded a suitable environment. The old man yielded to all her suggestions and paid all the bills. Her taste was ornate, but not very

pure. The great rooms were filled with colour
and decoration. Nothing was left untouched.
It was a restless, almost intimidating spectacle.
The eye roved from one glowing hue and
glittering point to another, without repose.
It seemed hardly lawful to sit down on these
satins and velvets. The polished floor menaced
the incautious foot ; the tables were inlaid ; in
the midst of it all you kept catching glimpses
of your own mortified countenance in plate-
glass mirrors. I like comfort and hate this
sort of thing, and felt a brutal longing to spit
on the floor and put my feet on the buhl and
marqueterie. As for fine art, there were clever
nude statuettes by French sculptors, and paint-
ings of warm Venuses, and I know not what
else ; and, in the most conspicuous part of the
drawing-room, a really fine full-length portrait
of Madame Hertrugge herself. She stood
facing you, in the act of removing a voluminous
cloak lined with swansdown from her white,

superb shoulders. She was represented in full evening dress,—red satin. It was a good likeness : almost too good. It might make a sensitive person blush.

Madame Hertrugge was white, red, and black. Her skin was white, her cheeks and lips red, her hair, eyes, and eyebrows black. Her mouth was beautifully formed, and firm, with a firm chin. Her eyes were rather full, imperious and ardent. She was overflowing with vitality. The hand which she extended to one in greeting was soft but strong, with long fingers. She was dressed in black, as became her recent widowhood ; but she had not the air of mourning much. She was sensuous, voluptuous, but there was strength behind the voluptuousness. You received from her a powerful impression of sex. Every line of her, every movement, every look was woman. And she made you feel that she valued you just so far as you were man.

You might be as nearly Caliban as a man can be, but if you were a man she would consider you. You might court her successfully with a horsewhip, but if she felt the master in you, and were convinced that you were captivated by her, she would accept you. It was ludicrous to think of the senile old merchant having married such a creature. In fact marriage, viewed in connection with this woman, seemed an absurdity. There was nothing holy about her, nothing reserved nothing sacred. I don't mean that she was not lady-like, as the phrase is. She knew the society catechism, and practised it to a nicety, but like a clever actress, rather than by instinct or sympathy. It was obvious that she didn't value respectability and propriety the snap of her white fingers, save as a means to an end, and if she were in the company of one whom she trusted intimately, she would laugh those popular virtues to scorn with her warm, in-

solent breath. As it was, all the forms and
ceremonies in the world could not disguise
her. Her very dress suggested rather than
concealed what was beneath it. She was a
naked goddess—a pagan goddess—and there
was no help for it. She made you realise how
powerless our nice institutions are in the presence of a genuine, rank human temperament.

And be it observed, that I am here writing
of her as a temperament, and nothing more.
I knew nothing of her former life and experience. I had no reason to think that her conduct had ever been less than unexceptionable.
But the facts about her were insignificant
compared with her latent possibilities. Circumstances might hitherto have been adverse
to her development : but opportunity—rosy,
golden, audacious opportunity was all she
needed. She certainly bore no signs of
satiety : she had nothing of the *blasé* air.
She was thirsty for life, and she would appre-

ciate every draught of it. She was impatient
to begin. And, contemplating her abounding,
triumphant, delicious well being, it seemed as
if she might maintain the high-tide of enjoyment until she was a hundred. It really inclined one to paganism to look at her. What
is all this gossip about morality and the *con-
venances!* I thought of Will Burlace and his
thermometer. Here is a woman; here is
human nature as it came torrid from the
creative hand. What else in the world can
stand a moment's comparison with it ? What
a race of cold-blooded pigmies are we become!
Let us eat and drink, and not die, either to-
morrow or the day after. I am a temperate
man, but she made me feel as if I had suddenly
drunk a bottle of fine old Madeira.

But, as I say, her behaviour was unexceptionable. She shook hands with me in
the quietest and most undemonstrative way,
and asked me politely how I liked Dresden,

and whether I expected to make a long stay. Then she turned and spoke briefly to Ralph, and we all sat down on the satin and velvet. She was between Ralph and me ; but I was directly opposite the portrait, and the glance it gave me, whenever I happened to look at it, did not harmonise with the kind of remarks (about the weather, the opera, and so forth) that the original of it was making.   On the other hand, although the remarks were out of character, the tones of the rich, full voice were in keeping ; and I listened to them, while replying to the words.

·   ' Where is Conrad ? ' asked Ralph, after a while.

' Oh,' she said, ' he's in his study, with Hildegarde.   Hildegarde is my daughter, you know,' she added to me ; ' though really there is not such a very great difference between us, in point of years,' and she smiled.   ' She and her brother have not met for a long time, and apparently they have a great deal to say to each other. But they will be in in a few minutes.'

'Miss Hertrugge has been living away from Dresden?' I said.

'She has been educated at a convent,' returned the widow. 'She has just completed her course, and will henceforth live with us. She is very charming—I am sure you will like her,' she added, letting her black eyes rest on me.

Somehow I did not feel complimented. The look was an appraising one. It seemed to say, 'Hildegarde would suit a person of your calibre well enough; as for me, I must have stronger meat!'

Indeed, I was inclined to agree with her. Merely to contemplate her was stimulus enough for me. I was content to let some more robust nature proceed further.

'She will make it less dull for you this

spring,' remarked Ralph ; and he added, with the quiet audacity which he occasionally exhibited, 'Mourning is a tedious business. One chief reason for wishing to keep some of our friends alive, is the dread of mourning them after they are dead.'

'Too much importance is given to the outward show, perhaps,' said Madame Hertrugge, after a moment.

'No doubt of it,' said Ralph. 'It is like most other social canons ; the fact that you are expected to comply with it makes you resent it. The way the social law puts its great bullying finger into our most sacred concerns is indecent. Birth, death, marriage, —it is the same in everything. We cannot even experience religion except in public, and with the aid of a batch of priests. The aim of society seems to be to turn its members inside out: and the more it succeeds, the greater hypocrites do we all become.'

' That sounds like a paradox, Mr. Merlin,' said our hostess.

' It is the natural revolt of human nature against force. Society insists on regulating our behaviour by averages ; we demand individual choice. Society being the stronger, we adjust the matter by obeying the letter and rebelling in the spirit. It is our only way of keeping the ownership of our own souls.'

' That,' observed I, ' is as much as to advocate hypocrisy.'

' Resistance to tyrants is obedience to God, —have you not that proverb ?' said Madame Hertrugge, taking Ralph's part against me.

' Yes, you are right,' she went on, ' we are all something that we try not to appear to be. But I can at least say for myself that I do not enjoy being a hypocrite. It stifles me : I am tempted to throw off the disguise.' She made a gesture with her beautiful arm—a gesture that quickened my pulse a beat or two. Her gestures, like everything about her, were graphic and vividly suggestive. If she were really to throw off the disguise, it would be a memorable sight.

At this juncture, Conrad came in, with his sister Hildegarde's hand in his.

The two stood together in the doorway a moment. There was very little family resemblance between them, except that Hildegarde's hair was tawny. Her eyes, as I judged, were hazel; they were large and exquisitely expressive. All her features were delicately moulded, and evinced great sensitiveness. Withal, there was a certain abstraction in her manner. It struck me that she would be keenly aware of all that passed before her, yet less through the ordinary channels of perception than by some sixth sense,—some instinctive apprehension. It acted from the depths within her, and penetrated to depths, ordinarilyc on-

cealed, within others. She would note the
false tone of a voice, and see through an
assumed geniality. If you loved her, she
would know it in spite of your best conceal-
ments ; if you were hostile, she would feel it
through your sultriest complacency. And, as
I afterwards found by experience, she often
divined the unspoken thought of her interlo-
cutor, and would even, at times, inadvertently
reply to that, instead of to what had actually
been said.

She was, compared with her step-mother,
as spirit to substance, and as light to heat.
Her complexion was fair and pure ; her figure
was slenderly symmetrical, and charming
with unstudied grace. There was something
strange about her which, at first, I did not
understand ; but at length I came to the conclusion that it was her almost total lack of
self-consciousness. This girl had no egotism.
Her observations, her reflections, her thoughts,

E

were of people and things outside herself. This, as is always the case, would give her singular power in emergencies. She would never say, ' What will be the consequence of this or that to me ? ' She would consider only the abstract result. Yet she would reverence noble qualities, and goodness, in herself, not less than in others ; not because they were hers, but precisely because she, in comparison with them, was nothing ; they would not be her goodness and ability, but goodness and ability themselves. ~~These gone~~, she would be no complying slave, but as stubborn at need as a martyr. You can defeat a person who says, ' I will have it so,' but the world cannot influence one who says, ' Right will have it so.'

But my observations upon Hildegarde did not proceed so far on this first evening. She bowed to Ralph and to me, with a pleasant, clear look, as her step-mother mentioned our names. In a few minutes, I was conversing with her and Conrad, while Madame Hert-rugge in another part of the room, was talking to Ralph. But both Ralph and Hildegarde were inattentive, and I saw each of them look at the other once or twice.

' Do you remember your own mother ? ' I asked her.

' Oh, I can see her,' she replied, turning and lifting her head a little.

' Memory, with some people, is almost like vision,' Conrad added quickly.

' This is a great change from the convent,' said I.

' I like it ! ' she returned, with a simplicity that made me smile.

' She and Catalina will be great friends,' remarked Conrad.

' Why, do you not wish it, brother ? ' demanded the girl.

' I forgot your eyes ! ' he rejoined with an

odd gleam in his own, and a comical twist of
his sardonic mouth.   He certainly had not intimated that he did not wish it.   'She has
more of her mother than of her father,' he
said to me.   'My father was almost as ugly
as I am, and clever—a good brain.   But an
ugly man ought to be strong, and there he
was lacking.   A woman could make a fool of
him.'

While he was speaking, Hildegarde rose,
and crossed the room to where Ralph and
Catalina Hertrugge were sitting.   It was a
point-blank interruption of a tête-à-tête that
had seemed to be interesting to at least one of
the parties to it.   If one has the nerve, or the
assurance, to go straight to the point in
society, such a one will leave the subtlest
schemer far behind.   I did not know whether
Hildegarde's manœuvre was more than an
accident ; but it evidently disconcerted the
other lady.   Hildegarde stood looking calmly

at Ralph, and not offering to say anything. Catalina, cut short in what she was saying, must have felt annoyed ; but she laughed, and motioned to the other to take a place beside her on the lounge. Ralph had meanwhile risen and drawn up another chair, and this Hildegarde accepted, replying, at the same time, to something Ralph said to her. In a moment Catalina exclaimed : 'But we are forgetting our tea !' and moving to the embroidered bell-rope, pulled it. Then she sauntered on, with that undulating movement of the hips which is so beautiful and so rare in women, showing, as it does, perfect suppleness and freedom of the waist and limbs,—she came on, I say, towards Conrad and me, and sank into a seat near us, the train of her dress coiling over her arched feet as she did so. The servant appeared at the door, and she ordered him to bring in the tray.

'Are you not afraid to trust Hildegarde

with so handsome a man as Ralph?' asked Conrad, with a saturnine grimace.

'She will amuse him, and he will benefit her,—he will teach her something,' Catalina replied ; and then, turning to me, ' I shall depend on you and him to help me with her ; I want to make a success of her.'

'And yet they abuse step-mothers,' said Conrad.

All this was entertaining, and the tea was brought in, and some flagons of Rhine wine also, and we became quietly convivial all round.   But it seemed to me that there were forces at work which might breed events that would be something more than entertaining. Two women and one man make mischief ; and Conrad appeared likely to take a hand, too.

CHAPTER IV.

SCHANDAU.

IT was several weeks before I saw either Catalina or Hildegarde again. It was then May,
one of the loveliest months of the year in
Dresden. The grass was soft and green, the
new leaves made a tender verdure on the
trees, and the lilacs were in bloom, and their
perfume filled the air with a benediction.
The sky was softly blue, enriched with clouds,
which are nowhere more beautiful in form
and colour than in the valley of the Elbe.
The river itself came swirling and rippling
down from amidst the distant hills, overflowing with the freshness and fullness of the
gracious season, and foaming against the dark

piers of the old hog-backed bridge that had
stemmed its current for centuries. The pro-
prietors of the river baths had begun to
construct their platforms and moor them out
in the stream ; and a wooden terrace was
being built on the bank beneath the walls of
the Bellevue Hotel, whereon, during the summer, innumerable beer-drinkers would sit
and imbibe the great German liquor in the
breezy shadow, with the water eddying and
sparkling beneath them. Now, also, the
open-air concerts at the Grosser Garten, and
at the Waldschlösschen, and other easily acces-
sible suburbs, were in full blast, enabling you
to hear the best of music at any time for five
cents. All the population appeared to be
parading about, ceaselessly loquacious and
smiling, in fresh bonnets and spring waist-
coats. Good old King John, still alive at
that epoch, might sometimes be met toddling
along the sunny side of the Schloss strasse,

with his old queen by his side, and a hench-
man or two in attendance ; in the morning
you might see Crown Prince Albert, accompanied by a lady who was too handsome to
be royal, cantering down the Hercules Allée,
through fretted sun and shadow. It was
spring, full of fresh days and sunny hopes.

One Saturday we made a party to go up
the river to Schandau. This is a charming
little village in a narrow winding valley,
about twenty-five miles above Dresden. The
village, beginning with a hotel at the river
bank, prolongs a line of leaf-embowered villas
for some half a mile along the brook side,
there ending in another hotel. You take
your meals beneath the trees, in the open
space in front of the hotel ; a band plays
there in the afternoon ; on either side are
precipitous cliffs, on whose sides trees miracu-
lously cling, and which are ascended by paths
zigzagging upward at practicable angles.

Schandau is the outpost of Saxon Switzer-
land, the loveliest little region in all
Germany.

The party was to include the three Hert-
rugges—Conrad, Catalina and Hildegarde,
and Ralph, Will Burlace and myself. This
was two cavaliers apiece for the ladies, which,
considering the excess of women over men in
Germany, ought to have been very satisfactory
to them. But at the last moment Conrad found
it impossible to go. As all our preparations
were made, and the day was fine, it was
decided to proceed without him. The cause
of his defection was a telegram he had received
at breakfast from one of the professors at
Freiberg, announcing an important meeting
to be held that day to consider the case of a
certain student, known to Conrad, who had
got into trouble. Conrad was at first inclined
not to comply with the summons ; but inasmuch as the boy's future seemed likely to

depend upon his attendance, he finally made up his mind to go. At parting he drew me aside and said : ' I don't feel altogether satisfied about this thing. The student is one of the steadiest in the school. I cannot understand his having behaved in such a manner. Will you do me a favour ? '

' With pleasure.'

' Well—keep the party together as much as possible. I shall feel more at ease if I know the young people are not getting too romantic. You are a man of sense—one can trust you ; but the others — ! '

' There is safety in numbers, professor,' I replied, laughing ; ' and under the circumstances, I do not regard what you say about me as a compliment. However, I will engage to see them all home alive this evening.'

He rubbed his chin, seemed to meditate for a moment, and finally turned away muttering something I did not catch. He took the train one way, and we the other.

In spite of his absence, we were a very merry party. Burlace gave the guard a thaler to lock the door of our compartment, which was a first-class one. The two ladies established themselves at the opposite windows, and just as the train started Catalina called to Ralph and asked him to disentangle the lace fringe of her scarf from one of the buttons of the cushion, to which it had somehow become attached. By the time he had accomplished this I had taken my seat opposite Hildegarde, and Burlace was on the other side of her; so there was nothing left for Ralph but to devote himself to the beautiful widow. But it appeared to me that no one was pleased with this arrangement except Catalina,—leaving myself, who would have been contented anywhere, out of the question. That is to say, Burlace wanted to be with Catalina, Ralph

wanted to be with Hildegarde, and Hildegarde
—to put the attitude negatively, as becomes a
young unmarried woman—Hildegarde did not
exhibit any marked preference for the society
of either Will Burlace or myself. As we had
a full hour's ride before us, this was, perhaps,
unfortunate. But the genius of Ralph was
equal to the emergency. He did not, indeed,
imitate the sublime example of Hildegarde,
on an occasion already described, and simply
and without excuse or explanation, change
his seat from where he did not to where
he did want to be : but at our first stopping
place, Pirna, he was suddenly seized with
a desire to speak to the guard, and since
the station was on Hildegarde's side, he
was obliged to come to that side in order to
satisfy his desire. What he said to the guard
I do not remember : but while he was standing with his head and shoulders out of the
window, Burlace took advantage of the oppor-

tunity to transfer himself to the place opposite Catalina, and then Ralph, finding
his retreat cut off, was, of course, obliged to
sit down by Hildegarde. So now we were
all happy except Catalina,—and myself, who,
as I have already explained, was the ac-
knowledged supernumerary and mere looker-
on. In this order we arrived at our destina-
tion.

After being ferried across the river to the
Schandau landing, we strolled up the lane by
the brookside to the hotel, and ordered our
dinner for one o'clock. We took this walk in
a group, the promiscuous character of which
was almost conspicuously, albeit tacitly, preserved. But at this point I abandoned for the
nonce my rôle of chaperon, and declaring that
I must and would have a bath (there are excellent baths in the hotel), I left my four
friends to fight it out, or flirt it out, as best
they might. They started off to ascend the

hill on the left, and were soon lost to sight in the bosky pathway leading thither.

I entered my bath, congratulating myself on my uninteresting and uninterested character. But though my heart was free, my curiosity and speculative instincts were awake, and I could not help wondering what would come out of this little game at cross-purposes. Too much weight might easily be ascribed to what I had noticed, and yet it was plain that the two ladies both preferred the same man, to wit, my friend Ralph Merlin. I could not blame them for this. Ralph was to poor Burlace as Hyperion to a satyr. But what would be the result of it ? Would Hildegarde be able to hold her own against so redoubtable and potent a beauty as Catalina. If the object of their rivalry had been any other man than Ralph, I should have doubted it. But Ralph, though human enough in all conscience, in spite of his trick of talking metaphysics and mysticism, was not a man to mistake an outside for an inside, still less to prefer the former to the latter ; and, moreover, he did not appear to be merely indifferent between the two women, but had betrayed a certain measure of preference for the strange girl with the hazel eyes. Catalina, then, was in so far at a disadvantage ; nor was her situation improved by the obvious fact that Hildegarde reciprocated Ralph's interest. In a matter of love, an unsophisticated maiden may sometimes prove more than a match for even a beautiful woman of the world and a widow. And Hildegarde had traits of character that would have to be taken into consideration by anybody.

Upon the whole, I was benevolent enough to be sorry that Catalina had not happened to take a fancy to poor Will Burlace. If it were not an ideal match, at any rate it was really preferable to one between her and Ralph. And after all, why should she be in such haste to

fall in love with anybody ? Only seven or
eight months ago she had a husband. It was
true that the deceased Mr. Hertrugge may
have won her not solely on his own merits ;
but some consideration was due to the poor
man's memory. And what would Conrad say
to such behaviour ? It was already evident
that he was not pleased about something ;
though whether it was to the marriage of his
step-mother, or that of his sister, that he
objected, I do not know. Neither was I aware
what power he possessed, if any, to oppose or
check the proceedings. But, again, possibly
—and I thought it quite possible--Ralph might
feel only an æsthetic or psychological interest
in Hildegarde, in which case a half at least of
the Gordian knot would be cut. By this time
I had finished my ablutions, and resuming my
garments, I sat down in the courtyard to await
the return of my friends, and the arrival of
dinner. It was not long before I heard voices

F

from the hillside, and among them the stentorian tones of Burlace, who seemed to be in a complacent mood. I was curious to see in what order the quartette would reappear. When, presently, they hove in sight, it appeared that fortune continued to favour Hildegarde thus far. She and Ralph were together, walking some twenty paces behind Burlace and Catalina. Nevertheless, Catalina was in high spirits—rather unduly high, I fancied. She was laughing and talking with Burlace, and looked positively glorious, with her complexion like white and red roses, and her eyes like black diamonds. I was conscious of a great and disinterested sympathy for her. What a pity that such a woman could not have her own way in everything! With so much of primal nature in her, she must be more good than bad. There was evil in her, of course, as there is in everybody; but it would come to the surface only if she were opposed, or injured, or disappointed. Why could not fate allow her to enjoy herself in her own way? It is singular how life often seems to provoke people—deliberately hound them—into being worse than they might be. Catalina would be all right if she were let alone. On the other hand, if she were crossed and driven into a corner, she was capable of serious mischief. As for Burlace, he was enchanted! He belonged to the class of people who are most sanguine at the moment when everyone else perceives their final discomfiture. Ralph and Hildegarde, like Dante and Beatrice, were happy but quiet.

The dinner was good ; and we had some Marcobrunner that was so inspiring that we were convinced it must be the original drink of immortality, from the famous Fountain of Youth. And yet, what did we want of the wine of youth? It was twenty years ago. I would appreciate it better now.

Every once in a while I caught a glance from Catalina's jubilant black eyes. What was in that woman's mind? Sometimes, too, I saw her looking at Hildegarde ; and then her regard became pre-occupied and dreamy ; it made me think of an Eastern empress, calmly watching the agonies of a dying slave. Yet Hildegarde was neither a slave nor moribund.

Coffee was brought, and we lighted our cigars. The sun had passed its zenith, and was shining up the narrow valley. The band appeared and began to play. But the music was too near and loud ; by common consent we rose, and sauntered down the shadowy path towards the river. On arriving there, Catalina pointed to a steep elevation on our right, covered by some small buildings, and commanding a fine view, and proposed that we should ascend thither. It is nothing to a party of young people to climb a mountain in

the evening of a day's outing.   Up we went,
bending to the arduous path, breathing deep,
and rejoicing as height after height was
gained.   Reaching the breezy summit, we
found there a tiny 'Restauration,' with
benches and tables in front of it, and intima-
tions of cool beer in the background.

We sat down on the benches, and were
waited upon by a neat and comely little
maiden, with her flaxen hair braided down
her back, after the manner of the Gretchen of
romance.   I, being otherwise mateless, entered
into converse with her, and she made cheerful replies to my questions.   There was a
little dome-shaped structure on the top of a
rocky knoll, overlooking even the height on
which we sat ; and I asked her what was kept
in it.

' Oh, that is the camera-obscura,' she said.
' Have you never seen one ? '

I had ; but camera-obscuras have an

abiding fascination for me ; and I wanted to
see this one also. Gretchen expressed her will-
ingness to do the honours of it ; I laid the
matter before the others, but none of them
were inspired by my enthusiasm, so I left them,
and went up with Gretchen into the mount of
vision.   It was an excellent camera, and commanded a vast horizon.   After causing the regular series of sights to pass across the stage,
ending up with our own party still seated at the
tables, Gretchen paused and asked me if I
were content.

I crossed her honest little palm with silver,
and requested her permission to remain in the
camera by myself for a while ; to which she
readily assented, and departed to her other
guests and duties.   I got hold of the cord that
moved the lens, and began to explore the neighbourhood at hap-hazard.   The silent but living
pictures, in the lovely colours of nature, suc-
ceeded· one another ; the trees waved, the

river ran, the little skiffs sailed to and fro
upon it ; an interminable freight train slid
along the track, with white steam puffing
from its engine. Once an eagle sailed
leisurely athwart the sky, without a pulsation,
of his long dark wings. I turned the glass full
upon the sky, which showed lakes and straits
of intense azure, between superb masses of
cloud, fleecy white and tender gray, like the
plumage of a sea-gull. Turning more to the
west, I saw there masses thickening and dark-
ening, and assuming here and there strange
tinges of yellow and green ; and towards the
remote horizon there was a whitish blue. A
thunderstorm was coming on, and setting in
this direction. As the frowning cloud wall
drew nearer, I could see lightning wriggling
across it.

The idea of watching a thunderstorm as it
painted itself in a camera-obscura pleased me
hugely; it combined the realism of nature with

the imaginative charm of a theatre. I directed the lens to the little restauration, in order to find out what my friends were doing ; but they had all vanished. Only Catalina's parasol lay upon one of the tables ; and Gretchen stood in the door of the house, glancing at the sky and the landscape. Had the others wandered off somewhere, or were they in the restauration ? I grasped the magic cord, and set off on a voyage of discovery.

CHAPTER V.

THE SPECTRE OF THE CAMERA.

THE nearer rim of the storm-cloud was now nearly overhead, and the body of the disturbance was but a mile or two distant, sweeping up the valley of the Elbe, and shrouding the lofty cliffs of Kœnigstein and Lilienstein in driving rain. I kept the darkest part of the cloud on the centre of my canvas, and watched its swift and majestic approach. The lightning was incessant, and showed blue and red as well as white, and the unintermittent roll and explosions of the thunder filled my ears. If my unfortunate companions had gone out into the woods, they would inevitably be drenched to the skin.

I surveyed my immediate surroundings for several minutes without seeing traces of any of them. The elevation to which we had ascended, following the general conformation of the region, was in the shape of an irregular butte, or table-land bounded on all sides by nearly vertical precipices. These precipices, however, were cleft by deep ravines and gullies, whereby access was gained to the summit; and the summit itself was only comparatively level—it was, in fact, rough and uneven, with loose boulders resting upon it, and everywhere a thick growth of pines and other trees. Narrow footpaths wound in and out from one point to another, but there had been no attempt to render the surface homogeneous.

From my high standpoint, I could command this limited space much better than any one below me, and I accordingly passed it carefully and systematically in review, with the assurance that I could not fail to discover

my friends sooner or later, if they were anywhere upon it.   By-and-by I was rewarded
by the sight of Catalina and Will Burlace,
who were standing . together beneath the
broad boughs of a pine, looking out at the
oncoming storm.

Presently Catalina turned to Burlace, and
seemed to be speaking to him ; he replied ;
they glanced up at the boughs above them,
and then again out over the valley.   I judged
that she had offered some suggestion, which
they had discussed, and to which Burlace
acceded ;. for a moment later he nodded his
head, left her side, and walked off at a brisk
pace in the direction of the restauration.   She
had doubtless asked him to fetch her an
umbrella, or a cloak, to protect her from the
rain.

I followed his course for a few moments,
as he alternately appeared and disappeared in
the windings of the path, and beneath the

overhanging branches of the trees. It struck
me that he was taking the wrong path, but I
was unable to apprise him of his error. I
returned to the spot where he had left Catalina ; but to my surprise, she was no longer
there. Had she left the tree for some more
effective shelter from the imminent downpour,
or for another reason? It suddenly struck
me that the errand on which she had des-
patched Burlace might merely be another of
her expedients to get rid of him ; and as soon
as he was out of sight she had transferred
herself elsewhere.

But this could only be a piece of wanton
mischief on her part, or it might even be co-
quetry ; for she had nothing to gain now by
hiding herself from him, except the certainty
of getting wet. It was not as if she were
plotting to exchange Burlace for Ralph, for
Ralph was not there. By the way, where was
he? and Hildegarde? she must be with him.

All this time the gloom of the great overwhelming cloud was deepening, and the savage
flashes of lightning made the intervals between
seem darker ; and the thunder was uninterrupted, booming and crashing and leaping in
heavy echoes from peak to peak of the hills,
as if giants were flinging vast boulders at one
another. The appearance of the surface of
the cloud overhead was awful and bewilder-
ing ; it boiled and eddied like an aërial
maëlstrom ; it was iridescent with lurid
tints, and pieces of vapour were ever and anon
torn off from the main mass and snatched and
twisted about this way and that in the fury
of the upper whirlwind. It was a terrifying
spectacle ; such a storm as this I had never
seen in Germany, and at so early a period of
the year it was unprecedented. I began to
fear that Ralph and Hildegarde and the
others might be exposed to a real danger.

'Just then a turn of the glass brought

Ralph into view. He was hurrying across the rough ground and through the wood, not attempting to keep the path, but making a straight line for the restauration. He was alone, and I could only suppose that he, like Burlace, had started to procure some means of protection for Hildegarde, whom he had probably left in some place of comparative shelter. The first breath of the gale had now reached the butte, but as yet not a drop of rain had fallen.

All at once, Catalina stepped out from behind a rock, directly in Ralph's path, so that he almost ran against her. He halted suddenly; and then I witnessed a remarkable scene.

A dazzling flash of lightning glared out, and simultaneously with it came an appalling crash of thunder. I saw Catalina, as if beside herself with terror or excitement, throw herself upon Ralph, and fling her arms round him.

Ralph was apparently as much surprised
at this as I was. But he instinctively put
his hands on her shoulders, and for several
moments she clung to him, with her face
against his breast. The gloom had closed
round them, but in another breath it was lit
up again, and she was looking up in his face,
and speaking passionately. He drew back a
little, but again she clung to him; all the
strength and fire of her nature were put
forth; who can tell what she said or intimated? The mere distant reflection of the
scene, from which I could not turn away my
eyes, revealed and concealed in quick and
irregular alternation by the electric flashes,
made my nerves thrill and my pulses beat.
Beyond a doubt this magnificent creature was
offering herself to Ralph; could any man
withstand the intoxicating onset of such a
spirit and passion as hers? And to all was
added the excitement and hurly-burly of the

great storm, as if the elements themselves took part in the tumult of her heart and brain.

It seemed to me that Ralph wavered for a moment. He would not have been human had he remained unmoved and in command of himself. To hear such love so told ; to feel her alive in his arms and pressed against him : to see that beautiful face so close to his that her lips spoke almost against his lips, and her eyes wet with wild tears and ardent with the flame of her desire looked into his own,—in such a situation virtue dissolves like snow in fire. Ralph bent his head towards her ; for an instant darkness closed them in ; and what took place in that instant I know not. But alas for Ralph, and for her !

The revulsions of feeling in such cases are as rapid as they are intense. I knew that Ralph did not love her, and that he had yielded to a passionate impulse only. And

having yielded, at such a white heat of emotion, the recoil would be inevitable and absolute. When I looked again he had unclasped
her arms, and drawn back from her a step ;
they faced each other so, and he was speaking.
As he spoke, at first she heard him defiantly
and wrathfully, standing erect at her full
height, with her head poised like a serpent's,
about to strike. Then some word of his hit
her hard ; she winced and her head fell ; she
half-raised her hands and shrunk as if to
avoid a blow. And then her arms dropped
listlessly to her sides, and the pose of her
figure expressed the apathy of despair. She
attempted no reply ; she did not lift her face :
and when he left her and passed on, she did
not turn to look after him.

Evidently, then, he had smitten hard ; and
few men could smite harder than he. And
he had killed something in her. Perhaps it
was pride ; perhaps it was something better

G

than pride. We are always wrong when we judge our fellow-creatures, and we are wicked when we condemn them and shame them, no matter for what cause. Possibly Ralph would have been less cruel had he not known in his heart that he too was accountant for a sin.

After Ralph was gone, Catalina moved, drew her shoulders together as if she felt cold, and passed her hands over her eyes. She took a step or two forward, and paused; walked a few paces in another direction, and paused again. She seemed hardly to realise where she was, or what she was doing. But presently a change came over her; some definite purpose had entered into her mind, and she had immediately become intent upon it, to the exclusion of all other ideas. At first I could not imagine what it was; but her course was taking her directly to one of the most headlong precipices, which plunged sheer downwards, five hundred feet without a break, to a chaos of tumbled rocks beneath. What should a desperate woman, whose love had just been thrust back on her with contumely, seek on the edge of a precipice ? The answer was terribly obvious. I was about to witness the suicide of Catalina, without being able to do anything to avert it. I was powerless as a man in a dream. She was in one world, and I in another, with no possibility of intercommunication ; and yet we were perhaps not more than three hundred yards distant from each other.

She was now within twenty paces of the end. A sloping terrace, some ten feet in height, descended to the rocky brink. At the top of the terrace grew two or three small evergreens, and just on the crest of the declivity was balanced a small boulder, about as big as a mammoth pumpkin.

When Catalina reached this terrace, she

stopped short, with a start, and then drew back behind the shelter of the evergreens. Here she crouched down and gazed ; and I gazed too.

On the very brink of the abyss, where the downward slope of the terrace ended, stood Hildegarde. She stood looking outward towards the storm, which filled the vast gulf before her. She was absorbed in the spectacle. She held herself proudly and exultingly, like some divinity of earth and air ; the fighting wind had loosened the fastenings of her tawny hair, and it streamed out behind her with a movement like leaping flame, and her garments fluttered like a rent sail wrapped on a slender mast. She raised her arms, as if to rise on wings and stem the gale.

Her position was one of imminent peril. A step forward—a loss of balance—and she would have been lost. But she was manifestly unconscious of danger, or indifferent to

it. Her nerves were not shaken : her heart
beat strong and full : her reserved and silent
nature was awake and rejoicing. It needs
planetary influence to arouse some souls, while
others expand themselves at the bubbling of
a tea-kettle. In spite of her logical danger,
Hildegarde was safe. I wondered whether ·
the storm alone was answerable for her ex-
altation, or whether Ralph also had been concerned in it.

Did the same thought come to Catalina at
that moment ? As I turned my eyes on her,
I saw that she had emerged from behind the
evergreens, and was creeping towards the small
boulder that was poised above the slope. All
the while her gaze was fixed intently on
Hildegarde, as a panther watches a fawn upon
which it prepares to spring. Catalina reached
the boulder, and laid her hands upon it.

Then I comprehended what was about to
happen. A vigorous push, such as Catalina

was fully able to give it, would send the boulder bounding down the terrace. Hildegarde stood exactly in its path over the precipice. It would strike her, and sweep her down to destruction. Catalina had changed her purpose from suicide to murder. Ralph had crushed her pride and scouted her love. She would see to it that Hildegarde did not enjoy his love either.

As I saw the wretched woman press against the stone, I involuntarily shouted out to warn Hildegarde of her fate. I might as well have appealed to the stars. My voice came impotently back to me from the black sides of the camera; and even had I been as near her as was her intending murderess, the reverberations of the thunder and the roar of the wind would have out-shouted my words.

The stone stirred and trembled on its fall. But before it could descend, a figure appeared

on the very verge of the gulf. It almost
seemed as if it must be standing on the empty
air ; it was on a level with Hildegarde, and a
pace or two to her left. How it had come
there was more than I could conceive ; an instant before, a glare of lightning had shown
the place vacant ; the next flash had, as it were,
brought him there—for the figure was that of
a man, and of one whom I immediately recognised. Its appearance and what followed
thereupon, all passed in the fraction of a
minute ; but it seemed to me that the new-
comer was more clearly visible than either
Catalina or Hildegarde ; the effigy cast by the
lens had a kind of luminous quality in it, as if
it had absorbed some of the electric light which
charged the atmosphere. The figure extended
his left hand towards Hildegarde, and beckoned to her with an urgent gesture. She, too,
evidently recognised him ; but manifested
little or no surprise at his presence.

The stone plunged downward ; but before it could reach Hildegarde, she had quietly stepped a pace to the left, and it flew past her harmlessly.   I saw Catalina throw up her hands and stagger back, with an aspect of terror ; but when I looked again for the apparition of Conrad Hertrugge, it had vanished.

CHAPTER VI.

MR. HERTRUGGE'S WILL.

SIMULTANEOUSLY with this strange event, the
rain, which had held off so long, rushed
down in a gray sheet, and blotted out everything. It rattled upon the roof of the
camera with a noise like the beating of innumerable kettle-drums. But I had seen
enough ; the spell that had kept me there
was broken ; I found the door and came
forth. The rain struck me like a shower-
bath, and I was soaked through before I
could descend the knoll to the level. The
first thing I saw was Ralph and Burlace
running off through the trees with waterproof
blankets in their arms.

I had no wish to follow them. I did not doubt that they would find Catalina and Hildegarde, and bring them safely back. I walked across to the restauration. Gretchen met me in the doorway with exclamations of concern and compassion. The Herr was so wet! The Herr would catch cold! Everybody would catch cold! Never was such a storm known. What was to be done? Oh weh! Oh weh!

I followed her into the kitchen, where I took off my coat and waistcoat and sat down before the cooking-stove. Gretchen trotted here and there, getting out dry wraps for the ladies, when they should return. I could think of but one thing—the appearance of Conrad on the cliff. By no means could I imagine how he could have got there. I had seen him depart in the train for Freidberg. It was an hour's journey from Dresden thither. The first train back to Dresden did

not leave Freidberg until half-past one in the
afternoon. Supposing him to have taken it—
which in itself was most unlikely—he would
have reached Dresden at half-past two. The
first train after that, from Dresden to
Schandau, started at half-past three, arriving
at half-past four. I looked at my watch; it
was now twenty minutes to five. Granting
that he had been on that train, it would have
been impossible for him to have been ferried
across the river and to have ascended the hill
in less than twenty minutes; and five minutes
had already passed since I saw him. According to my reckoning then, the event fell
at least fifteen minutes short of being a
physical possibility. The only way out of
the mystery was to suppose that Conrad had
chartered an engine specially to convey him
hither. But to charter an engine is by no
means so simple an affair in Germany as it is
in America. Moreover, what conceivable

motive could have induced Conrad to take such a step ? He could not have foreseen that his sister was to undergo any peril.

Apart from all this, however, the conditions under which I saw the figure were inexplicable. The peculiar luminousness and distinctness which characterised it ; the position in which it stood, apparently on nothing ; and the circumstances which I now recalled, that its garments, in the midst of a gale that was bending the pine trees like grass, hung down unmoved, as if in an atmosphere completely calm ; all these things combined to fortify the mystery. I should have put down the appearance as an hallucination, due either to the disturbed state of the air, or of my own mind at the time ; but it had evidently been seen also by both Hildegarde and Catalina ; the former had obeyed its gesture to move to one side, and the latter had been overcome with fear. Besides, the figure had not appeared to me directly, but through the medium of the lens of the camera ; and I had never heard of an hallucination presenting itself in that manner.

My meditations had reached this unsatisfactory conclusion when I heard voices and steps, and turning, I saw my four friends entering the kitchen, convoyed by Gretchen. The rain, meanwhile, had ceased, having been as brief as it was violent ; the heavy clouds were breaking away in the west, and the roll of the thunder sounded like the cannon of some great battle far to the north and east. Catalina and Burlace came first, laughing and talking ; then Hildegarde, whose face had unusual colour and animation, and finally Ralph, whose straight black eyebrows lowered over his eyes. He was the only one of the four who seemed to be out of spirits.'

'At last I have had my wish,' exclaimed Catalina, throwing off her blanket. 'I have always wanted to be out in a thunderstorm without an umbrella, and now I have done it. Nothing could be more refreshing !'

'But what about dying of pneumonia ?' said I.

'Dying ! I am not going to die, Monsieur. I am going to live and be happy ? I am already younger than I was this morning. I have bathed in electricity as well as in rain-water.'

'And yet you would commit suicide ?.' said I.

She became pale in a moment, and gazed at me with a sort of stealthy consternation. Her lips parted, but she did not speak.

'It is nothing less than suicide,' I continued, ' to think of going home in those wet clothes. You are on the brink of a precipice. Draw back ! '

'What an old raven you are !' put in Burlace, with his rough voice. 'You are always for plaguing folks ! Madame Hertrugge is all right. She is dressed in woollen, and the rain won't hurt her. Still, madame, if you would like to put on one of Gretchen's gowns while your things are drying——'

' No, not I.!' she replied, taking breath and recovering her self-possession. 'Besides, we must take the train in half an hour.'

' I have a better plan than that,' remarked Ralph. ' The steamboat starts in half an hour too, and you and Miss Hildegarde can have a stateroom on that. You can go to bed during the run home, and by the time you get there your things will be dry.'

' Oh, to be sure, Hildegarde is delicate !' returned Catalina, with a touch of mockery in her voice ; ' you are quite right to consider her, Mr. Merlin.'

' I wish I had a horse here, I would like to ride,' said Hildegarde.

' Twenty-five miles on horseback would be a little too much, after to-day,' replied Ralph,

looking at her with undisguised tenderness ;
' we are answerable to Conrad for you.'

'By the way,' said I, glancing carelessly at
Catalina, 'have any of you seen Conrad this
afternoon?'

Catalina started perceptibly, and again the
colour left her face. She dropped her eyes,
and the hand which she put up to smooth
back her hair trembled.

'I believe you've got a chill in spite of
your woollens, Madame Hertrugge,' said
Burlace. 'The boat will be the best thing,
after all. What's that you say —saw Conrad?'
he added, staring at me with a grin of amazement. 'There's nobody here that I know of
can see from this to Freiberg. What are you
thinking of?'

'Well,' I said, 'he may have been here in
spirit, at any rate. If we are going to take
that steamer I think we had better be getting
off.'

We all rose and made ready to go. Hildegarde came up to me as I stood a little
apart from the others, and looked at me
anxiously.

' Can you see spirits ? ' she asked, in a low
voice.

' Ralph and I were debating the other day
whether spirits could be seen,' I replied. ' I
believe he argued that they could not. What
is your opinion ? '

' Spirits . . . perhaps not,' she said slowly.
' But I fancied you might mean . . . however,
it is no matter.'

' The ancients used to believe in tutelary
spirits, or something of that kind, whose office
it was to warn them of danger, and advise
them. I should not be surprised if some
being of that order watched over you—some
aërial Conrad, you know, who filled his place
when he was absent.'

Her eyes became very penetrating, and

she was about to reply, when Ralph came up to her and took her arm under his with an air of ownership that meant something. Burlace had Catalina ; I brought up the rear. Matters were plainly coming to a head ; but I felt ·by no means prepared to guarantee that the head would be an altogether peaceable and agreeable one.

We arrived at the wharf at the same time as the steamboat, and started on our downward journey, which would last until long after dark. We succeeded in procuring rooms for the ladies, and they disappeared. Burlace went off to drink a glass of Schnapps in the cabin ; and Ralph and I obtained permission to sit and smoke in the engine-room, where the heat from the furnace made us steam like a laundry.

' I wish we had stayed at home,' I remarked, after a period of silence.

' There is no day of my life that I would

be willing to substitute for this,' Ralph returned, emphatically.

'Wait until you hear what Conrad has to
say about it,' was my answer.

He smiled and said : 'You think yourself
a good guesser.'

'I suppose you have already obtained
Madame Hertrugge's consent ?' said I.

'Oh, I don't care to make a secret of it,'
he returned, leaning his head on his hand and
fixing his grey eyes on me. 'I have reason
to believe that I shall marry the loveliest
woman in the world. At the same time, there
is no need to make it a matter of common
talk, until the preliminaries are settled.'

'And until her year of widowhood has
expired.'

'Her year of widowhood! What the
mischief do you mean ?'

'Madame Hertrugge's husband died less
than a year ago.'

He gave me a keen look. ' What is your motive in suggesting that I contemplate marrying Madame Hertrugge ? '

' Why not ? Do you mean to say that you have never done or said anything to lead her to think that she was not indifferent to you ? '

He hesitated, and his eyes darkened. 'You have no right to ask the question,' he replied at length ; ' and I would be justified in parrying it. But I prefer to admit that there has been a moment in my intercourse with her which I wish could be wiped off the record. As to marrying her, there never was any question of that. She can't marry.'

' Why can't she ? '

' On account of a clause in her husband's will.'

' Oh ! He forbids her to marry under certain penalties ? '

' If she marries while Hildegarde is still un-

married, she forfeits the enjoyment of the late
Mr. Hertrugge's fortune.'

Here was a whimsical complication.
Catalina could not marry until Hildegarde
was married. But since it was Ralph that
Catalina desired to marry, and since, when
Hildegarde was married, it would be to Ralph,
it was evident that Catalina would never marry
at all.

' Love may be secondary to money in her
estimation,' I said.

' You must ask her about that yourself.
The will also allows her to marry in the event
of Hildegarde's death.'

' Mr. Hertrugge was a donkey,' said I.

I was half minded to tell Ralph what I
had seen that afternoon. Many and many a
time since have I regretted that I did not.
But he had shown himself so restive under
my questions that I was reluctant to meddle
any further ; besides, had not Hildegarde

undergone her peril and escaped ?   But what a sinister light this news threw upon Catalina. It was hardly doing her an injustice to say that probably nothing would induce her to give up her fortune ; she had married an old tradesman of seventy to obtain it ; and she was of a temperament that needs wealth as much as other people need air and water. And yet she had offered herself to Ralph. Nor was that the worst. Her attempt to murder Hildegarde no longer appeared as simply the wild revenge of a jealous woman. That fool, her late husband, had deliberately put a premium on his daughter's death ; and Catalina, in removing her, would have combined with her revenge a shrewd stroke of business.

'Shall you remain here after your marriage ? ' I asked presently.

'I shall go back to America.'

'Well,' I said, 'I wish you joy with all

my heart, and I think the sooner you are married and off the better.'

'Thank you,' said Ralph. 'And now, if you are dry, suppose we go up on deck'

It was a lovely evening Nothing of importance happened during our journey. Catalina and Hildegarde made their appearance just before our arrival at Dresden; and the first person we saw on the wharf was Conrad, in flesh and blood.

CHAPTER VII.

BURLACE'S LUCK.

A FEW days later, as I was sitting in my room, with the implements of my work around me,—a sheet of drawing-paper stretched on a board, a saucer of Indian ink, a box of drawing instruments, and a set of calculations for the construction of toothed wheel gear,—with these, and a volume of Heine's 'Reisebilder' (which I happened to be studying at that moment, in order to familiarise myself with the language),—there came a loud knock at my door. People stamp their characters upon everything that they do ; and there was a freedom, a self-opinionativeness, and a lack of consideration for the

feelings of others about this knock, that at
once informed me who was outside. I closed
the volume of Heine, put it under a pile of
drawings, took up my drawing-pen, dipped it
in the Indian ink, and said :

' Come in, Burlace.'

He had already turned the latch, and now,
he bounded in, with his big boots, his small
cap, his pipe, and his noisy voice.

' Sit down,' I said, in a preoccupied voice.

' Don't hurry, old man.' he returned,
cheerfully ; ' I've got the afternoon free.'

' Lucky fellow !' said I, with a sigh.
' Now, I've got work enough on hand to
occupy me for a week.'

' In that case,' he answered, ' you may as
well call a halt right here. You work too
hard, anyway. I believe, if it wasn't for me,
you and Ralph would both of you get your
brains addled. I never come in but I find
you grinding away as if you were on the

track of the Philosopher's Stone. You make a big mistake. I go in for independent thinking. A book is only a man's opinion, after all; and one man's opinion is as good as another's, and sometimes a little better!'

'What have you been thinking about lately?' I inquired, putting down my pen.

'I've been wondering, for one thing, what you and Ralph find to admire in that fellow Conrad. I consider him a beast.'

'And his step-mother, too?'

'If it's all the same to you,' said Burlace, gruffly, 'I would thank you not to insinuate anything against Madame Hertrugge. She is without exception the finest and most intelligent woman I ever met.'

'Intelligent, is she?"

'Well, rather. Why, look here! I am working a good deal just now in the direction of investigating the origin of diseases, with a

view to developing the theory of prevention
by inoculation. It will be proved, some day,
that contagious and epidemic fevers, cholera,
and a lot more of the scourges, are the work
of microscopic germs in the atmosphere and
in water. But the entire subject is at present
in a very obscure condition, and some of the
best men we have, who ought to keep their
minds open, you'd think, are still too timid
and bigoted to take it up.'

'What has that to do with Madame Hertrugge's intelligence ?'

'It has just this to do with it : that I
happened to mention the subject to her the
other day, and she was interested in it at once.
She asked me questions that would have done
credit to an expert ; she saw the point of all
my explanations at half a glance ; and when
I told her some of the results of microscopic
investigation, she made me promise that I
would let her have a look at the things

herself. If you don't call that intelligence, I'd like to know what you do call it!'

'I might find another name for it, perhaps,' said I. 'At any rate, I might suggest a predisposing cause.'

'What do you mean?'

'No harm, I assure you. But you know what the poet says,—"Love lends a precious seeing to the eye!"'

'What right have you, or any man, to assume that I am in love with—with anybody?'

'It's the other way, my dear Burlace. One can't help noticing what is before him; and you must be aware that Madame Hertrugge's preference for your society has been imperfectly concealed, to say the least of it.'

At this Burlace's large mouth relaxed, and a ruddy hue showed itself beneath the bristly growth of his beard. 'Of course,' he remarked, 'that is a thing I can say nothing about. A

disinterested observer would see more than I
could. Women are strange beings ; when you
expect most of them, they are away off, and
when you have given them up, round they
come again. But I suppose there are various
ways of intimating the same thing, and there
may be something in your idea that her interest is quickened by a favourable regard for me.
That would be natural, and at the same time
it would detract nothing from the fact of her
intelligence.'

'On the contrary,' said I, laughing, 'her
intelligence is sufficiently vindicated by the
fact of her favourable regard for you.'

' Look here—if you are chaffing me——'

'Nonsense, Will,' I cried out, testily, ' why
shouldn't I chaff you ? What are love-sick
idiots good for but to be chaffed ? I am not
in love with your Madame Hertrugge, nor she
with me. Do you expect me to leave my
Heine—my drawing, I mean—for the privi-

lege of listening to your rhapsodies ? Why
don't you go and talk to her ? You began by
calling a friend of mine a beast, and now you
want me to sing the chorus to your amatory
drivel. I am not tuned to that key.'

Burlace knocked the ashes out of his pipe
on my table, and grinned. ' That's all right,
old fellow,' said he. ' You certainly have
been left out in this arrangement, and between
Ralph and me, you come to the ground. Well,
I'm not going to tantalise you with the spectacle of my good fortune ; but when I say that
Conrad is a beast, I mean it. If he doesn't
look out, he will get a piece of my mind one
of these days.'

' That will do him more injury than any
of your inoculations for physical disease. But
do empty yourself of your message, if you
have one, and leave me in peace ! '

' That fellow Conrad,' continued Burlace,
imperturbably, ' actually had the face to insult

Madame Hertrugge in my presence. He told
her to remember that her late husband had
lived long enough to know her character ; and
that however much her disposition might in-
cline her to play fast and loose with other men,
the terms of his will would suffice to put them
on their guard against her. What do you
think of that ? '

' It was pretty plain speaking. What did
she say ? '

' She showed the dignity and self-possession
that only a lady is capable of. She told him
that she valued the friendship and sympathy
of an honest man more than any consideration
that he (Conrad) was capable of appreciating :
and that rather than have her free actions
misconstrued, she would willingly surrender
what he was pleased to call a check upon her
liberty.'

' Do you know to what Conrad re-
ferred ? '

'I didn't at the time; but she told me afterwards. It seems that senile old imbecile of a husband of hers provided in his will—'

'You needn't trouble yourself to tell me,' I interposed; 'I know it already.'

'Oh, you do! Conrad has been warning you off the premises as well.'

'I never exchanged a word with him on the subject.'

'I understand!' said Burlace after staring at me for a moment. 'The information came from our friend Ralph. I've nothing against Ralph; he's all right. And if he carries out his intentions, I shall be under obligations to him. You know, of course, that as soon as he becomes the husband of Miss Hildegarde there will be nothing to hinder Madame Hertrugge—'

'And does she favour the match?'

'Of course she does. She has taken pains to become acquainted with Ralph, and to test

his character, and she has become satisfied
that he is unobjectionable.'

' I haven't noticed that she has taken pains
to throw the young people together, however,'
I remarked.

' How could she, stupid ? ' demanded
Burlace. ' Don't you see the delicacy of
her position ? If she were to appear as a
promoter of the affair, wouldn't Conrad and
all the other fools in the world scream out
that she was scheming to retain her fortune ?
She felt it to be her duty, as Hildegarde's
only friend of her own sex, to investigate the
character of any suitor for her hand ; but,
beyond that, she was obliged to restrict
herself to — what they call benevolent
neutrality ! '

This view of the case struck me as being
so pathetically ludicrous that I could not
help laughing. After what I had witnessed
at Schandau, the interpretation of Catalina's

I

behaviour as ' benevolent neutrality ' was ini-
mitable.   ' I should have thought,' I said,
' that she would have applied to you for a
certificate of Ralph's availability.'

' That happens to be precisely what she
did,' he returned, complacently.   ' I told her
that Ralph was a trump in all respects, and
that I was convinced that he and Hildegarde
were born for each other.'

' You did ! '

' I did ; and she said—with a tone and
look that I am not likely to forget in a hurry
—that she had perfect confidence in my
judgment and perception, and that I had
taken a load of anxiety off her heart.'

' Burlace,' said I, ' I'm a friend of yours ;
you bore me horribly sometimes, but I like
you, and if I knew a good sensible girl whose
happiness and well-being I wanted to insure,
I should tell her to get you to marry her.
And I am now going to give you an even

greater proof of my friendship for you by doing something that will probably make you my enemy for life.'

' Go on ! ' returned Burlace, without evincing, I must say, any violent symptoms of agitation.

' Well, I advise you to pack up your trunks and go back by the shortest route to Chicago, and to forget all about Germany and everybody you ever met there. As sure as you stay here, you will get into the worst scrape that any honest man ever got himself into yet.'

Burlace looked at me intently for several moments. My tone was serious, as my feeling was, and he saw it. He answered me with a gravity and dignity that touched me not a little.

' I'm sorry you said that,' he observed, · but I'm not your enemy for it, because I don't believe you're the man to talk loosely

on such a subject. You meant it well ; but—
well — I love that lady, and if any harm
comes to me on that account, I'm ready and
willing to take it as it comes. If she cares
for me, I should feel myself so lucky that a
misfortune would only put things straight.
But if you have anything against her, I give
you notice that I will not listen to it. I believe in her ; I believe there is no purer or
better woman in the world ; and whoever is
against her must be against me—sorry as I am
to say it to you, old man.' The voice of the
honest, pig-headed fellow faltered at the last
words, and he ostentatiously began to fill his
pipe and hunt in impossible places for a match.

I felt as if there might be tears in my own
eyes. My affection for Burlace had never
been so strong as it was then ; and he was
caught in a net from which there could be no
escape that was not more or less disastrous.
Catalina meant to use him as a tool to carry
out her purposes on Hildegarde and Ralph.

What her purposes were, or how she would
employ Burlace, of course I did not know, but
I could not doubt the intention. She had
been checked once ; she would profit by
experience, and so devise that there would be
no check the second time.

It would be useless in Burlace's present
state of mind, to tell him the story of my
hour in the camera at Schandau. He would
not credit it, even if he consented to listen to
it. I could only keep such watch as circumstances permitted on her future movements.
But even that was less my affair than either
Ralph's or Conrad's. There were probably
no secrets between them, and they would
take such measures as they deemed necessary.

It sometimes seems as if we could help
one another, in this world, only in minor and
insignificant matters. When the real pinch
comes, we are powerless, and can only observe
the inevitable approach of destiny.

CHAPTER VIII.

A DRAMATIC TRIUMPH.

In Germany, the ceremony of betrothal is an event of greater social importance than it is here ; you often see the announcement printed in the newspapers, and it is made the subject of comment and congratulation among relatives and friends.   There is something pretty and patriarchal in the idea ; though, society not being quite patriarchal at the present day, I am not sure that the results are especially beneficent.   Privacy is sometimes better than picturesqueness, in an artificial age.

However that may be, the news of the betrothal of Hildegarde Hertrugge and Ralph Merlin was made known, about this time, to

interested persons ; and an invitation was
issued to a select few to meet the young
people at a reception given at Madame
Hertrugge's house. I received a card, written,
a little to my surprise, by Catalina herself ;
and, as a matter of course, Burlace was
there.

This was the nearest approach to a social
festivity that had been given at the house
since Mr. Hertrugge's decease, and I suppose
people were anxious to see how the widow
would conduct herself. The purport of the
late husband's will was generally known, at
least among the nearer friends of the family,
so there may also have been some speculation
as to whether the consequences of the antici-
pated marriage were likely to be availed of
promptly, or whether the handsome Catalina
would prefer to postpone indefinitely the for-
mation of fresh ties. But it was agreed that
she was fortunate in getting released so early

from what must have been at best a somewhat annoying stipulation.

I came rather late, and the company had
already assembled, and had got over the first
formalities and uncertainties of the situation.
The drawing-room was comfortably filled;
there was a number of officers, with the air of
immaculate and insolent self-complacency that
is the general characteristic of German warriors, and has become still more marked since
the war with France than it was before; there
were several professors, friends of Conrad,
and, for the most part, acquaintances of my
own ; there were a few nondescript persons of
the male sex, presumably relatives ; there
were a dozen or twenty homely women, two
or three good-looking ones, and one conspicuously beautiful, who, I need not say, was
no other than Catalina herself.

As for Hildegarde and her lover, though
they were in the unenviable position of being

the cynosures of the occasion, they did not
seem to mind it much ; their love for each
other enabled them to rise superior to circumstances. They stood near each other, as we
ordinarily measure distance, yet remote enough
for lovers, since two or three paces and twice
as many people intervened between them.
but across this gulf of time and space they ever
and anon threw a proud glance at each other,
as much as to say : ' My love, I am yours ;
the world cannot part us ! ' It is wonderful
and delightful how this dawn of love
between two worthy human beings always
leads them back to pure, primitive emotions,
so that they are sure that they are the first,
since Adam and Eve, to discover and enter
the vale of Paradise. ' No one ever loved
before ! ' is the refrain of their thought ; and,
indeed, there is always a hope—a possibility
—that now at last the time may have come
when the world, and our sad human life in it,

is to undergo transfiguration, and begin again with those two lovers. The world grins at them and calls them silly ; but the lovers know, with the deepest and soundest of all knowledge, how tragically and grotesquely silly is the grinning world. Merely by love, and by that only, can all the problems of political economy, all the abuses of society, all the miseries of mankind, be solved, reformed, alleviated. ' Only be like us,' the lovers say, ' and you will be whole ! ' The world grins ; but ah ! how glad and grateful its poor old wizened heart would be, if love could but gather power really to conquer it and lead it captive ! You may know that this is true by observing the eyes of elderly people, when the little hugging arms of infancy are around their necks ; and by noticing with what jealous delight the world follows the fortunes of any lovers who have had the wisdom to be silly all their lives. The vic-

tories which the world enjoys and celebrates
are never its own, but always those of its
opponents over itself.

One does not often meet with a pair of
lovers having a more assured air of victory
than Hildegarde and Ralph wore that evening.
But Hildegarde was infinitely the more at-
tractive object of the two, not only because
she appeared this evening in the consummate
flower of her maidenly loveliness ; but because
love, for her, was a self-surrender, whereas for
Ralph, as for all men, it was more an acquisi-
tion.   He adored and reverenced her, no
doubt ; but he was also conscious of the pride
of possession—of having won the treasure for
his own, to keep and defend against all rivals.
Such a feeling, in its final analysis, is selfish.
But in the maiden's love there is no selfish-
ness.   Her longing and ambition was not to
possess him, but to be possessed by him ; to
give herself to him so entirely that nothing of

herself should be left that was not his, and him ! Their union should mean, not a linking together, but the merging of herself in him. She grudged herself even the happiness that his love wrought in her ; she would have all the happiness his, but could not make it so, because the more his happiness was increased, the happier must she be.   So hers was the divine inspiration, and her fair face was radiant with a purer light than can ever shine in the countenance of any son of Adam.

She was dressed in feathery white ; her eyes had the soft, mysterious darkness that characterises hazel eyes in moments of deep emotion.   There was more colour than usual in her cheeks ; it had an opaline quality, coming and going with a thought or a look. For ornament she wore the opal ring that Ralph had given her,—an exquisite stone, trembling with celestial fire.   But, somehow, it made me sad to look at her.   Life was not what she thought it was. Many cruel sorrows would come to her, and the light that was in her eyes to-night would grow faint and infrequent. It seemed almost a pity that the attainment of such felicity as this should not be the immediate prelude to what those who do not love call death. The valleys of shadow through which we walk do not always give strength. Often, they benumb and bewilder, and only a forlorn parody of the young traveller who sets forth so blithely arrives at last on the shore of the unknown river.

I took Hildegarde's hand in mine, and made my formal good wishes ; but she seemed far off, not from any voluntary remoteness on her part, but because I did not inhabit the sphere of her existence. As for Ralph, his measureless content was trying to mere friendship. 'I hope you don't think you deserve her,' I said to him.

' There is no measure for measure about it,'

he replied. 'The only place where a man approximately gets his deserts, is hell ; and he probably imagines even that to be heaven.'

'What is heaven ?' I asked.

'The marriage of the good and the true,' said he. 'It is the marriage that makes heaven—not either of the contracting parties. That is where my chance comes in.'

'You had better say nothing ; nothing you can say fits the occasion.'

'Which occasion ? My betrothal, or this reception ?'

'True,' I admitted ; 'and I am in the wrong as usual. There are times when association with one's kind is almost indecent. If a fairy were present at my betrothal, I should ask her for the cup of invisibility.'

After this unsatisfactory dialogue, it was a pleasure to turn to Catalina. There was no remoteness in her sphere ; she was on the earth, and of it. Her behaviour was exactly

what it ought to be—assuming the situation
to be what it externally appeared. She was
pleased at her step-daughter's happiness, and
yet there were some traces of solicitude in the
look she occasionally bent upon her, as if she
were not yet quite sure that all was for the
best. As regarded herself, there was a certain
reserve of manner, conveying the impression
that she was far from being in haste to claim
the rights of emancipation that Hildegarde's
marriage would confer upon her, but rather
meant to substitute her own volition for the
restraint lately imposed by her husband's
decree. Her mood, therefore, was one of
cheerful gravity; gravity being the background, and cheerfulness the outward ornament.

Inasmuch as she had struck me, when I
first met her, as being one of the most elemental persons I had ever seen—a woman of
a primeval type, experiencing and rejoicing in

the strong but simple passions that lie at the basis of human nature—I was hardly prepared to find her so accomplished in dissimulation. But, after all, dissimulation is itself an elemental trait. Animals dissimulate to gain their ends ; the bird whose nest is beneath your foot tempts you with the pretence of a broken wing, and the crocodile lies like a log until you are within reach of its jaws. Besides, jealousy and revenge are quick and effective teachers ; and there is a histrionic quality in women of the Catalina kind which facilitates their assumption of sentiments and expressions alien to their real ones. Catalina was evidently a natural artist in this respect.

'Love is a melancholy spectacle,' I said to her—for I too felt impelled, by magnetic sympathy perhaps, to reflect her dissimulation —'it promises so much and performs so little. Would you be willing to change places with that poor girl ?'

'You are too cynical,' she answered with a smile. 'Any woman might be proud and glad to be loved as Ralph loves Hildegarde. If I were melancholy, it would be because, for me, the time for that has gone by.'

'I would not hear your enemy say so!' returned I. 'If you have no more to do with love, it is you who must háve decreed the estrangement. And,' I added with an audacity that I myself could not but admire, 'had I possessed Ralph's mysterious faculty for winning hearts, I should have chosen the perfect flower, rather than stand the hazard of the bud.'

'If you possessed the gift, possibly it would amend your judgment,' she said, sending out a gleam of genuine anger from her black eyes. Then, with a sudden change of tone and manner, she touched my hand lightly with hers, and added, 'Love me, if you

K

will ; and we will learn wisdom from each other.'

Mockery though it was, it made me realise her seductive power. ' I am afraid ! ' I said, smiling.

' Afraid ! of what ? '

' That you would lead me to the edge of the precipice and push me over.'

' Ah ! ' said she, slowly. We looked at each other for a long moment. ' Why not push me over ? ' she asked at length ; ' you are the stronger.'

' But is there any need ? ' I returned.

' Ah ! ' she said again, in a different key.

Burlace was always hovering in her neighbourhood, and at this moment he approached, probably in response to some private signal: She turned from me, and I moved away. I had not intended to quarrel with her, and no benefit to anyone was likely to come from our little bout ; but the truth was, these attacks of mine were prompted by an instinct of self-defence against the influence she exerted over me. I am not considered generally susceptible ; but I felt a peril in her propinquity, and gave up Burlace for lost.

' All goes merry as a marriage bell, Professor,' I said to Conrad, seating myself beside him on a settee. ' What think you ? Will the example prove contagious ?' and I allowed my eyes to rest meditatively on Burlace.

' Your acuteness is greater than your judgment,' said he. ' Some people can be frightened into harmlessness ; but veiled threats, which you are so given to employing, only stimulate others to more dangerous activity. Pardon my frankness ; but I have a difficult affair on my hands, and a rash word, however well meant, might set the odds too much against me. You understand me, don't you ?'

' In your present sense, perhaps ; but—'

'Well, never mind the other senses,' he interrupted. 'Did I ever tell you, that the telegram I received the other day, summoning me to Freiberg, was a deception. The emergency it spoke of was a pure invention.'

'Who—'

'No matter who sent it. I mentioned it because you may have some reason to think that I am able to act effectively in predicaments that would find other men helpless. I don't deny that such may sometimes be the case. But at other times, perhaps quite as important, I am as liable to be caught napping as the stupidest man you know. If I had been clever enough to see through the telegram, for example, there would have been no necessity for the phenomenon that occurred afterwards.'

This was the first time that anything had passed between me and this extraordinary man on the subject of the apparition at Schandau.

Indeed, I had not spoken of it to any one; and if I was not surprised that he nevertheless knew what I had seen, it was only because nothing in which he was concerned could surprise me.

' You will not object to Ralph's taking her to America as soon as they are married ? ' said I, letting the mysteries go.

' Let us get them married first,' he replied, and even as he spoke there was a commotion and then a cry, at the upper end of the room. Every one rose; but Conrad had already made his way to the centre, whither all attention was strained. When I got there I found him with his hand on Hildegarde's pulse. She was reclining, half supported by Ralph. Her eyes were partly open, but she was evidently unconscious.

' It is the excitement—she has fainted,' said Catalina's voice close to my ear. I turned sharply and saw the profile of that beautiful face, as she gazed steadily at the pale, inanimate girl. 'Bring her to my own room,' she said, quietly. 'I will take care of her. It will soon be over.'

'Not so soon as you think!' said Conrad, looking up at her. A green light seemed to flash out from his eyes, and his thin lips receded slightly from his white teeth, in a grimace that cannot be described as a smile. If Catalina's sentence had borne a double meaning, so did his rejoinder, and the two foes had joined battle.

. The sympathetic bystanders saw only an episode familiar enough in ball-rooms, rendered a little more interesting than common by the fact that the young lady who had fainted was she in honour of whose betrothal they were assembled. They murmured their compassion for her, and for her handsome lover. But Ralph, after the first few moments, had become as cold and impassive as marble, as if he had read the fateful writing on the wall, and interpreted it. His gaze was bent with intense concentration upon Hildegarde's face; one would have said that he was willing his own life to substitute itself for hers. But he was isolated from the rest of the world; nothing coming thence could reach him.

'She'll come to all right; give her air and a whiff of hartshorn!' cried out Burlace, encouragingly. 'Don't you fret, old man; there's no danger!'

'Poor boy!' murmured Catalina, with a secret smile; 'it was a shame to spoil his happy evening. It was so pretty to see their delight in each other!'

Ralph rose to his feet, lifting Hildegarde lightly in his arms; the throng of spectators fell back, and he carried her out of the room, accompanied by Conrad. Burlace was about to accompany them, when Catalina arrested him by a glance.

'We won't make too much fuss about it,' she said, speaking partly to him and partly to the company. 'My step-daughter is accustomed to these attacks; she is delicate, and studied too hard in the convent. She will be as well as ever to-morrow, and her brother and Ralph are quite competent to take care of her.'

'I trust it will prove as unimportant as Madame Hertrugge thinks,' observed one of the professors, beside whom I happened to be standing. 'At the same time it did not appear to me like an ordinary fainting fit. A new disease has been diagnosed lately, very obscure and difficult in its features; it is heralded by abrupt spells of unconsciousness, accompanied by certain peculiar symptoms, which I seemed to recognise in the present case. We are endeavouring to investigate its origin by the aid of the microscope; but, so far, without any very satisfactory results. If one could only make experiments on the human subject! I wish some disposition, looking that way, could be made of criminals convicted of capital offences.'

'Is the disease you speak of fatal?' I inquired.

'No cure has yet been discovered,' he replied. 'Its duration is from two to three days. It appears to be painless, and produces little or no change in the external aspect of the subject, nor has dissection yet afforded any conclusive evidence as to the precise cause of death in the circumstances.'

The guests were taking their leave. Catalina was bidding them good-bye, with a comfortable smile and cheery word for each. 'What a woman she is!' I heard someone say. 'She is much more anxious about that poor girl than she pretends; but she will not allow her guests to be discomposed!'

At last, my time came to say good-night.

'What!' exclaimed Catalina, smilingly, 'are you, too, going to allow yourself to be frightened away? I shall owe Hildegarde a grudge for this!'

'You must permit me to say that you have managed this affair admirably,' I returned. 'It has been an artistic and personal success. And yet—there are so many slips between the cup and the lip—I hardly know whether my congratulations may not be even now premature. Have you no misgivings?'

'Come to-morrow!' she said, holding out her hand.

I took her hand. It was warm, firm and soft. Her eyes were clear, composed, triumphant. She felt no remorse, still less any fear. She was perfectly natural. She had met with an obstacle, and she had removed it. She had suffered a rebuff, and she had requited it. All is fair in love and war.

It was a long time before I saw her again, under very different circumstances. But, among all the times and phases in which I have seen her, the picture of her in my memory, as she appeared at this moment, remains most distinct. It was the most characteristic; there was more in it than in any other, of the real woman that she was.

CHAPTER IX.

THE PENTAGON.

I CALLED at the Hertrugge's house on the following day, to inquire as to the condition of Hildegarde, and was informed by the servant that she was still in bed. I saw none of the inmates, and as Ralph was not to be found in his own lodgings, I inferred that he also was with her. I then attempted to get hold of Burlace, but although I had good grounds for believing that he was in his room when I went to see him, his presence was denied at the door. Nothing remained but to wait for news to come to me.

On the evening of the third day, as I was standing on the old bridge that connects the

Altstadt with the Neustadt, looking down at
the current which eddies for ever against the
stone abutments, some one entered the little
semi-circular recess that I occupied, and stood
beside me.

I looked up at him—it was Ralph—and
was about to ask him how Hildegarde was,
but his face apprised me that a calamity had
happened.

'She is dead,' he said, after a moment,
'and I am on my way to London. I do not
care to stay for the funeral.'

'What did she die of?' I asked, mechan-
ically.

'Of a disease affecting the circulation. I
believe it has not been classified yet. Among
the many new inventions nowadays, there are
some new diseases.'

'But it is recognised as a disease?'

'Yes.'

'How did she get it?'

' As she might have caught a cold, or the smallpox. By the act of God, as the lawyers would say.'

' What shall you do in London? '

' Go to a hotel, I suppose. I have no plans. There is nothing to be done but to wait. How to make the time pass most quickly is the question. It is becoming tedious already.'

' How are Conrad and—' I hesitated.

' Conrad and Catalina are very well, I believe,' he answered, speaking, as he had done from the first, in an apathetic and list-less tone, as of a man physically and mentally weary, but no longer a prey to any emotion. He added presently, ' Catalina had no reason to be my friend, or Hildegarde's either; but I am bound to say she has been kind and sym-pathetic throughout. Conrad seems to dislike her; but her only fault, as far as I can see, is

that she is herself, and that is one common to
all of us.'

We leaned side by side upon the stone
parapet, looking down at the stream. I did
not think it expedient to make any remarks
'proper to the occasion.' Hildegarde was
dead; Ralph's life was a blank; I was sorry.
We both knew these facts, and talking about
them would benefit neither of us. What he
had said about Catalina had evidently been
sincerely meant, but it surprised me. For
though it was true that I had never told him
of her attempted crime at Schandau, yet I had
not expected Conrad to be as reticent; and if
he had known that, he would scarcely have
failed to suspect her hand in this case also.
Why had not Conrad told him? Did Conrad
himself acquit her? 1 could not believe it;
his silence must have had some motive which
I was not in a position to understand. At

all events, since he had not spoken, I had no cue to speak.

I contented myself, therefore, with making some suggestions looking towards my joining him, in the course of a few weeks, in London. I had previously made up my mind to leave Dresden after he and Hildegarde were married. I had spent over three years in somewhat desultory studies, and I did not care to remain after my chief friend had departed. Ralph made no objection to the proposal, though neither did he profess any particular gratification at it. His ailment at present was inability to care for anything. Our talk, frequently interrupted by silences, drifted into generalities, and finally he roused himself and said he must be going. Curiosity prompted me to say, at the last moment, ' Are you sorry that you met her ? '

' Oh, no,' he said slowly. ' I shall meet her again. I feel no absolute separation ; if

I die, I shall accommodate myself to it. The
conviction that our parting is only temporary
makes it easier to bear in one way—the higher
way ; but harder in another. As it is, I count
the days ; but one does not count towards
eternity.'

' And are you no more inclined than you
were to try the resources of Spiritism ? '

He shook his head. 'I certainly don't
wish to have Hildegarde parodied by the first
wandering disembodied courtesan who happens
to scent my bereavement. That would be
the way to lose her. As long as I keep her
image sacred in my soul, I am safe ; but if I
allow it to be manipulated and polluted by
sensual impostors—I might as well have cast
her living body before a herd of swine.'

' But what if there be no future life ? ' I
persisted.

' Then there is no life at all. And if our
belief that there is a life here be an illusion,

L

then it would be only reasonable to expect the illusion to continue after the illusion of death. I have no anxieties on that score.'

We shook hands, and went our several ways. I saw him cross the bridge, with his measured, but elastic step, and a slight swing of his shoulders from side to side, that would have revealed him to me among a thousand. Gradually the throng on the sidewalk intervening, rendered him indistinguishable; and I plodded home in low spirits, and with gloomy forebodings.

I do not belong to that numerous and respectable class who derive a certain gentle satisfaction from funerals. When my friends die, I would rather think of them as they were, and as I hope and believe they are, than associate them with any thought of the effigy in the undertaker's box. Accordingly, I made up my mind not to go to Hildegarde's funeral; Ralph himself had avoided the dis-

nal ceremony, and I had no reason to suppose that Conrad would notice my absence, or be flattered should I be present. Moreover, I did not like the idea of meeting Catalina there ; whether her look should be undisguised triumph, or of hypocritical grief, it would be equally unlovely. So I sent a note to Conrad, saying that I should be out of town on the day of the solemnity, and expressing the regret I sincerely felt at his sister's death.

To my surprise, he appeared at my lodgings the next morning. He seemed in his usual spirits, and, indeed, imported a lightsome tone into the conversation that struck somewhat discordantly on my ear.

'Unless you really have business that demands your absence from town to-morrow, my dear fellow,' said he, 'don't think it necessary to go on this account. Believe me, I fully understand your reluctance to put in an appearance on the occasion ; if I had my way, I would willingly omit the ceremony altogether. If people believe in a future life, they ought to be glad, instead of sorry, at the death of a friend ; or if they feel a selfish sorrow, they ought, as Christians, to suppress the exhibition of it. If, on the other hand, they believe that death finally ends all, what is the use of lamenting the irrevocable? Let them put it out of their minds as promptly as possible, lest they invite the unpleasant reflection that they themselves will soon be blotted out of existence also.'

'I am not altogether of your way of thinking,' I replied. 'It is right to pay respect to the memory of the dead. We would desire it when our own times come.'

' Ah, that is the point!' exclaimed Conrad, smiling. 'Stroke me, and I'll stroke you! But how absurd it is! Of what avail to your dead flesh and bones will my conventional respect be—or any other respect for that matter? As for your soul, if you concede yourself a soul, it will have other things to claim its attention than the length of its earthly acquaintances' faces and the breadth of their hatbands. No! the whole business is the remains of a savage superstition, to the effect that the ghosts of the dead haunted the scene of their corporeal existence, and executed vengeance upon those who failed to express a proper poignancy of grief at their departure. Given the superstition, the ceremony was at least intelligible ; but that it should survive the superstition is idiotic! '

' Possibly the superstition had some basis in fact,' I remarked.

He gave me a peculiar, quick glance, the significance of which I did not comprehend. It was as if he were questioning how far I spoke seriously.

' That, at any rate, is not the prevailing impression,' he returned presently, ' nor does it seem likely, on the face of it, that the ghost of Hildegarde could make itself very terrible to anybody.'

I made no answer, and, after a pause, he said, ' However, I didn't come here to discuss funerals in the abstract, but to beg a little favour of you.'

' I shall be glad of the opportunity of doing you one.'

' It is simply to walk over to my house with me for a moment. I have something I particularly want to show you. No!' he added, with another smile, ' you will not see my beloved step-mother. Her grief is far too absorbing to admit of her being visible even to you. So—will you come?'

I put on my hat and accompanied him to his house. Opening the door with his pass-key, he conducted me through a passage to another door, on passing through which I found myself in his study.

I had never before been admitted to this room, and I looked round me with some curiosity. It was singularly bare of the ordinary appurtenances to the retreat of a student. There was not a single book to be seen anywhere, nor any writing materials. The walls were of plaster, tinted a dull red ; no pictures decorated them, but in their stead there were sundry geometrical diagrams drawn with black and white lines. They conveyed no meaning to my mind. The ceiling was blue, of the same tone as the walls ; and there were waving lines of some obscure pattern traced on it. On a table, poised upon a slender stand, stood what I at first took to be a solid sphere of crystal ; it was in reality a spherical globe, filled with a transparent liquid, from which, occasionally, proceeded rays of pure azure light. The plan of the room was a pentagon. On the floor at the north end was a block of solid metal, apparently iron ; it also was pentagonal in shape, and a yard in di- ameter and a foot in thickness. From the ceiling directly above it was suspended the largest horse-shoe magnet I ever saw. A half- open cupboard revealed some steel and silver instruments, some glass tubes and retorts, and several bottles of various sizes containing coloured liquids. Finally, the angle of the eastern corner of the room was concealed by a voluminous curtain of black velvet ; and in the western angle, behind the glass sphere, was a full-length plate mirror, in a broad black frame.

'Now we are at home !' observed Conrad, closing the door behind me. 'No one can enter here without my consent. You may say that nobody would care to on any terms ; but I can be pretty comfortable here, in my own way, when I choose. Sit down and try a cigarette. I will be ready in a moment.'

He passed behind the black curtain as he spoke, and I seated myself in a chair and lit

one of the cigarettes he had offered me,
wondering the while what his object could
have been in bringing me there. But the
flavour of the cigarette was highly agreeable ;
it had an effect upon the mind at once sooth-
ing and clarifying. I have sometimes awak-
ened in the hour before dawn and found my
intellectual faculties in a similarly calm and
potent state. The smoke from the burning
tobacco, rising in the still air of the room,
was drawn by imperceptible currents into
strangely graceful lines and figures, recalling
those which the stricken chords of a piano
produce in fine sand, sifted over a sheet of
paper and placed within the instrument. I
remember ascribing the phenomenon at the
time to some subtle influence proceeding from
the great magnet.

I sat with my head thrown back against
the cushioned chair, abstractedly watching
these shifting forms, until I could almost im-

agine that they were observing some intelligible principle in their movements. I was just in the mood to weave some fanciful extravaganza upon this notion, when my attention was diverted by Conrad's voice, and looking round, I saw him standing beside the curtain, with his hand upon it He beckoned me to approach. I rose and went to him at once, and passing behind the fold of the curtain that he held aside for me, I found myself in a sort of shrine, lighted in some manner not obvious to me, but with a very soft and pleasing radiance. This radiance was concentrated on a sofa, set against the wall ; and on the sofa, clad in the same feathery white dress that she had worn at her betrothal party, lay the figure of Hildegarde, asleep.

CHAPTER X.

LIFE AND DEATH.

'What have you done?' I exclaimed, with
an involuntary impulse, turning from this
spectacle to gaze in Conrad's face. I felt as
if I had been unawares entrapped into as-
sisting at some uncanny exhibition of necro-
mancy.

Conrad's green eyes sparkled. 'After life's
fitful fever, she sleeps well, does she not?' he
said, in an ironic tone. 'What disturbs you,
my dear fellow? Have you ever seen a more
beautiful *cadaver*?'

'Is this Hildegarde, or an image?' said I.
I had been greatly startled, and I believe
there was an idea in my mind that Conrad

had made an effigy of his sister in wax. Either that, or some mystery.

He gave a slow laugh. 'That is the question that divides critical opinion at present,' he replied. 'Is this all there is left when we die? or is it but an image of what has been? What think you?'

I looked more steadily at the figure, and finally, overcoming my first reluctance, bent down and examined it. There could be no doubt that it was no waxen image, but simply the dead body of Hildegarde, neither more nor less. It lay in so natural a pose, however, and the illusion of quiet sleep was so perfect, that I could not help expecting to see the bosom rise in a long breath, and the great eyes open. But the dead never return to life, though it sometimes seems as if they easily might.

'The difference is not so great, after all,' remarked Conrad, replying, as he often did, to

my thought instead of to anything I had said.
'She seems to sleep ; and if you imagine that
it is sleep and nothing more, does it not
amount to the same thing ?'

'You had better ask Ralph that question,'
I replied.

'Ralph is not ready yet to be philoso-
phical,' said he, smiling. 'He was inclined
to be extravagent in his first demonstrations,
and it was for that reason that I persuaded
him to leave at once. When the first shock is
over, he will be safe ; and then he can return
and look at her without risk.'

'He has no thought of returning,' I said,
'and even if he did, the body would be in its
grave, and decay have set in.'

'There will be no decay in this case,' returned Conrad. 'I have made a pretty tho-
rough study of the science of embalming, and
I can affirm that I have not only fathomed all
the secrets known to the ancients on that sub-

ject, but I have made several independent dis-
coveries of my own. This body might remain
precisely in its present condition—barring accidents, of course—for an indefinite number of
centuries. She would be still fresh and young
when Ralph is tottering on the extreme verge
of old age; and he might return in some
future reincarnation (if the Buddhist theory
be true), and still find her as you see her at
this moment.'

'It is an ugly thought,' said I. 'I rather
wish that the body might disappear as soon
as the soul leaves it. At all events, let it
return to dust as soon as the process of nature
allows. What possible object can there be in
keeping it ?'

'In the majority of cases there would be
no object, and my opinion would agree with
yours. But as regards Hildegarde, there are
other considerations. I am interested in certain rather curious investigations touching the

connection between the soul and the body.
There are facts that seem to indicate that so
long as the body is preserved in its inte-
grity, the soul cannot altogether abandon
it. Ordinarily, the soul soon passes into
states where all possibility of communication with it ceases ; but, on the hypothesis to
which I allude, it might not be so inacces-
sible.'

'This is horrible !' I exclaimed. 'Do
you mean to say that your scientific curiosity
would lead you to bind the soul of your
own sister to the neighbourhood of the world
from which death has liberated her ! It
would be impious ! What end could justify
it ?'

'You had better ask Ralph that question,
he replied, repeating my own words of a few
minutes before. 'And if that be not enough
you might make the inquiry of my beloved
step-mother, Catalina !'

I stared at the man with an emotion not far removed from absolute fear.

' Do you seriously pretend to such powers as these ? ' I asked.

' I can hardly be said to claim a power, if I avail myself of natural laws,' said he, composedly ; ' and whether those laws be generally recognised or not, does not alter the case. What I have just suggested does not approach the abnormal so closely as did the incident that occurred at Schandau a few weeks ago.'

I turned away, feeling a little giddy, though whether by reason of the tenor of Conrad's remarks, or for some more concrete cause, I hardly know. But Conrad took me gently by the arm, and led me out of the shrine.

' Your nerves are a little off their centre,' he said, pleasantly, ' but luckily I have something here that will set you right in a moment. Come, sit down here.'

As he spoke, I felt a rush of cold air over my head and neck. I was sitting, not on the chair, as before, but on the pentagonal block of iron at the upper corner of the room. The rush of air came from above, apparently from the magnet. For a moment I felt a stifling sensation, and tried to rise and cry out, but I could do neither; an irresistible weight pressed me downward, and my muscles would not obey my will. I thought I was dying, and felt the agony of it; but then, in an instant, the agony and struggle ~~was~~ over, and *we* a delicious sense of lightness and power took their place. The cold rush of air was no longer cold, but had an exquisite, vivifying effect, as if life itself, from the pure original source, were pouring into my veins. The vitality thus communicated, though intense, was calm and deep; it prompted to no

M

physical activity, but caused thought and consciousness to enter an interior plane, where they acquired an immense development of scope and penetration. I sat still, and seemed to possess the world.

From my present point of view, looking from the upper or northern angles of the pentagonal room toward the opposite or southern side, the whole room appeared to arrange itself in a significant manner. The geometrical diagrams were no longer a mere complexity of unmeaning lines, but combined to form the words of a secret, whose purport solved the ratio between man and nature. The subtile angles of the walls, so perplexing at the first impression, now strengthened the expression of the mystic diagrams, and also suggested that semblance of life in inanimate objects which one finds in the architectural systems of mediæval Italy.

A delicate gray film of perfumed smoke,

similar to that which I had lately drawn from the cigarette, began to climb upwards from some concealed point behind me, and, marshalled by the magnetic influence, to move in sinuous courses across the dull blue of the ceiling. I presently perceived that these smoke wreaths harmonised by a sort of affinity with the eccentric curves that were inscribed overhead, and draped them, as it were, in aërial substance, as flesh drapes the human skeleton.

Meanwhile, the room gradually darkened, or appeared to do so to my eyes ; but the darkness did not prevent the forms on the walls and ceiling from continuing to be visible, though this may have been due merely to the existence of the impression already produced on the retina. The effect of the darkness, at all events, was to cause the solid sides of the room, and the roof above, to seem to dissolve and melt away, until I felt like one

poised in the depths of space ; but instead of
terror, the situation wrought in me an un-
speakable exhilaration and security.   I recognised in the diagrams, the orbits of the planetary system, in which wheeled several worlds
whereof science has given no account ; they
were at immeasurable distances, outwardly
estimated ; but, gazing at them with the eye
of thought, I could in a moment perceive
every detail of their glorious structure and
economy.   The smoke wreaths bent downward and took shape as the great spirits of
the elements ; they held their awful counte-
nances averted, but I saw that the iron pentagon on which I sat was upheld at each corner
by their right hands.   Whither they bore me
I know not, or whether they but held me motionless in the centre of the universe.   I had
no fear ; only perception.

All was still veiled in a transparent
gloom ; but presently a light like a star was·

kindled in the west, and gaining power, began to send forth azure streamers like those of the Polar lights, which throbbed and fell and rose again, increasing more and more, until the planets, and the long arcs of their courses, and the remote recesses of the heavens, and the forms of the awful spirits that encompassed me, were flooded and glorified with the great radiance, and emerged like the soul from the mysterious womb of prenatal being into the living existence of humanity. Accompanying this change was a sound of music, growing and multiplying, sweet as the warbling of Æolian harps, and strong as the thunder of oceans plunging over bottomless precipices. Every sense dilated and vibrated, receiving and concentrating the infinity of sights and sounds in the scope of individual intelligence; so that I was the universe, and the universe was I.

With the recognition of this truth the

vision of space receded, the outlines of the
spirits vanished, and the harmonious tumult
of the music culminated in a voice, loud and
yet still, speaking the creative word : ' Come
forth, and be ! ' I was again in the pentagonal chamber, sparkling now with the azure
lustre of the crystal globe, which kindled the
magnetic currents into living rainbows.
Looking in the mirror, I saw the black
curtain reflected there tremble and part, and
from within emerged the form of Hildegarde,
dead no longer, but alive and erect. Her
eyes had the distraught expression of one
aroused from deep sleep. There stood she
who had died three days before, breathing
and conscious. I saw her image in the glass,
but I could not turn my head to see the
reality which the glass reflected.

Her eyes bent themselves upon me, and
recognition slowly dawned in them. She
seemed about to speak ; but, as her lips

parted, they grew pale, and her eyelids quivered and dropped. The black curtain waved, and she sank backwards and vanished behind its folds. I heard a long sigh, and nothing more.

The azure lustre of the globe grew dim and dimmer, and faded out utterly. There were whispers and soft sweeping movements, and light echoes like departing footsteps. Then came a confused whirring in my brain, growing louder and louder, and again the sickening tremor of the heart, and the struggle for breath. I crouched down, and pressed my hands over my face.

'You are all right again now,' said the voice of Conrad, speaking in a brisk and cheerful tone. 'Perhaps the current may have been a little too strong. The effects are very similar to those of hashish, are they not?'

I looked up.   Everything was as it had been at first.   But Conrad's face was as white as a sheet, and his green eyes scintillated with conscious power.

CHAPTER XI.

LED BY A SPIRIT.

As soon as I could complete my arrangements to do so, I left Dresden and went to London. What I had experienced in Conrad's chamber may have been partly or wholly a dream or illusion of the senses, similar to the visions of opium and hashish eaters, as Conrad himself had intimated. And though I sometimes inclined to this view, at other times I could not reconcile it with the intensity and permanence of the effect produced upon me. No doubt I had fallen into an abnormal state, and much of the surroundings of the event were pure hallucination. The cigarette which Conrad had given me may have been drugged;

and I could only conjecture what might be the effects upon the brain of such magnetic or electric currents as his arrangements enabled him to produce.   But the two central events of the experience,—that I had seen Hildegarde dead, and had afterwards seen her to all appearances alive,—these things I could not dislodge from my mind.   I could not but believe that Conrad—for what end it was vain to ask—was indulging in practices which in old times would have brought him to the stake.   Whether his results were achieved by sheer witchcraft, or by some development of the principle of galvanism, were questions into which I did not care to enter ; in either case I considered them brutal and unholy, and I was resolved to tell the whole story to Ralph.   He could claim, and would doubtless enforce the right to protect the remains of his dead mistress from outrage.   At any rate, I felt bound, as his friend, to let him know

what was going on, and so place him in a
position to take what course he might deem
best.

The funeral took place before I left town,
and though I did not attend as an invited
guest, I took means to satisfy myself that
Hildegarde's body was in the coffin, and that
the coffin was safely deposited in the handsome tomb which the late Mr. Hertrugge had
had built for the accommodation of himself
and his posterity. This was so far satisfactory,
though, of course, the gates of the sepulchre
would be no barrier to a man like Conrad,
either physically or morally.

Ralph had given me his London address,
and I called there the evening of my arrival;
but he had left several days before. London is
a bad place to hunt for a person in; but I happened to know that his bankers were the same
as mine, so the next morning, I made inquiries
there. I then learned that Ralph had joined

an expedition commissioned to 'develop' certain unknown regions of Central Africa; and his steamer was already several hundred miles on her way to her outward port.

I had a passing impulse to go after him, for I was feeling rather unsettled myself; but I thought better of it upon reflection. It was a hundred to one that I should not overtake him; and even if I should chance to run across him in the wilds of the Zambesi, and spin my yarn to him, it would hardly be within his power to take up his march forthwith to Dresden, nor to get any satisfaction when he arrived there. Accordingly, I gave up all thoughts of the matter, contenting myself by addressing a letter to him at Natal, on the chance of his finding it there; and then I allowed the whole subject to sink into the latent regions of memory, and occupied myself with other pursuits and interests.

The very first rumours that came to hand

concerning Ralph's expedition, after it had passed beyond the limits of regular communication, were to the effect that it had met with disaster. A tribe, supposed to be friendly, had turned out quite the reverse, and the explorers had all been murdered. Such was the information supplied by a native attached to the expedition, who came back alone to Natal. Nobody believed that the catastrophe was quite as bad as that; the native undoubtedly exaggerated; the European members of the expedition were more likely to have been carried into captivity than slaughtered. But practically, one fate was about as bad as the other; for although, on the one hand, captivity admits a chance of escape, yet on the other hand a man who is dead has no further suffering and ignominy to endure. Though I did not admit it to myself, I presently came to the conclusion that Ralph was dead. It was painful to think of him as a captive ; and it was a fascinating subject of speculation whether his spirit had met Hildegarde's in the other world, and had found happiness with her.

My affairs took me to the United States ; I remained there over a year, chiefly in the western and north-western regions. I came into business relations with some English capitalists, who were interested in mining stock, and at length I found it expedient to return to London to confer with them. Reaching New York on my way eastwards, I put up at a hotel near Madison Square (my travelling expenses were defrayed by the English syndicate), and after a shave and a change of clothes, I walked out under the trees of the square. It was late of a warm June afternoon. In the centre of the square were benches, surrounding a circular fountain basin. I sat down on one of these benches, noticing as I did so the preoccupied attitude of its only

other occupant, a lean, athletic, middle-aged
man, with a short stiff beard, and black hair,
partly grizzled. A wide-brimmed Panama
sombrero was pulled down over his forehead ;
he leaned forward, with his elbows on his
knees, and his chin in his hands, gazing intently at—nothing. I took him to be a
wealthy Cuban or Mexican, meditating over
the lost Spanish empire, or wondering how
Dolores was getting along in his absence. I
suppose I looked at him rather oftener than
he thought necessary, for he suddenly roused
himself and turned an impatient glance upon
me. But his expression at once changed, and
he said with a smile :

'You are at your old tricks still ! Is there
anything in the world that can escape your
eyes and your knowledge ?'

'You are not Ralph Merlin !' I said.

'No,' he answered, 'but I used to be.'

I will not attempt to detail our talk ; I

am finishing a story, not beginning one. He
told me how his party had been attacked;
how he was wounded and captured; how he
had been assigned as a slave to a certain
powerful chief; how he had ultimately acquired such ascendancy over the chief and the
tribe, that he was requested to take the reins
of government into his own hands, to which
he assented; and to marry the retiring chief's
daughter, to which he demurred. He drew an
amusing picture *spretæ injuriæ formæ,*—how
the sable queen pursued him with her spite
and jealousy,—'my ill-luck followed me even
to mid Africa!' he added with a smile,—
until she made his life a burden to him; and
whereas, but for her, he might have settled
down to pass the rest of his life among these
savages, as it was, he determined to escape.
The story of this retreat of one man through
a thousand or more miles of pathless and hostile country was at least as interesting as the

celebrated Anabasis of the Ten Thousand
described by Xenophon. And when, at last,
he could exclaim with the old Greeks :
' Thalassa! Thalassa!' he found himself on
a part of the coast very remote indeed from
that on which he had landed nearly eighteen
months before. He had fallen in with a
Portuguese vessel bound for Ceylon, on a
rambling roundabout voyage ; she was run
down in mid-ocean by a British liner on the
way to Australia ; at Melbourne he had taken
passage on an American ship going to Hono-
lulu, and thence he had journeyed by the
regular steamer to San Francisco, and so
across the continent to the bench in Madison
Square where I found him.

This tale, as related by Ralph, was of absorbing and various interest, and lasted us
back to the hotel, through dinner, and well
into the evening. But, all along, I had a
feeling that Ralph was leaving something out,

N

and that this something, moreover, embodied the real gist of the whole matter. Again and again, there came a gap, or an abrupt transition in the narrative; or he would begin a sentence, and leave it uncompleted, and say another thing altogether. Now, I wanted the whole story.

' Are you going to complete your circuit of the earth?' I asked him. 'I am on my way to London; and we might run over from there to Dresden, and look up Conrad.'

The room—my sitting room at the hotel—was almost dark; we had not lighted the gas, and the only light came through the transom over the door. At the moment I spoke, I noticed a faint but unmistakable perfume in the room, as of some ethereal spice. Ralph had made no reply to my suggestion; and after his silence had lasted a minute or two, I turned to see whether he had fallen asleep.

No ; he was not asleep. He was sitting erect in his chair, leaning a little forward. In the dim light I could see that his great gray eyes were wide open, and the heavy black brows somewhat lifted. There was a sort of solemn ecstasy in his expression ; his gaze was directed intently towards the eastern corner of the room, which was occupied by nothing that I could see but a tall mahogany wardrobe. It was not at the warbrobe that Ralph was gazing, nor at anything else visible to normal eyesight. His whole soul was in the look ; and he was utterly unconscious of me, and of everything material in his surroundings. His lips moved ; he seemed to be speaking, but with an inward voice that carried no sound. He moved his head as if signifying assent ; a moment later the rapt expression faded out ; the peculiar fragrance ceased to be perceptible ; he passed his hands across his eyes, shifted his position in his chair, and said with a half laugh, 'I'm afraid you think me dull company ?'

'Anything but that!' I replied. 'But—we were not alone just now.'

'Did you see anything?' he demanded, so quickly and imperatively as to show that he was deeply startled.

'I did not see what you did,' returned I, 'but I saw you see it.'

He got up, struck a match, lit the gas, and took a turn or two about the room. 'Well,' he said at length, resuming his chair, 'you have stood so near me in certain crises of my life, that I may as well let you into my secret —especially as you have probably half guessed it already. But there is more to it than that. For the last year, or thereabouts, I have suspected that I am insane ; I should be nearly certain of it, but that I am neither more nor less insane than I was at the beginning. Now

I shall be very glad to have the dispassionate opinion of a man like you on my case.

'Just now, I saw Hildegarde and conversed with her. I saw her as plainly as I now see you, though the gas was not lighted then. By no test that I am able to devise could I distinguish between her reality and yours, for instance. I see her, I hear her, she is even sensible to my touch—or so it seems to me. During her presence, no doubt enters my mind that it is not Hildegarde, her very self; and yet, immediately before and after, I am as well aware as you are that the thing is utterly impossible. Hildegarde's body has been for nearly two years in the grave; her spirit must long since have passed through the spiritual world, and entered heaven as an angel. Therefore this vision must be a sheer mental hallucination, not based on any spiritual truth, but a spectre of insanity. I have argued it out a hundred times, and can come to no other conclusion.'

'This is not the first time you have seen her, then?'

'No, not by many. Her appearances have been the central fact of my life since I first resolved to escape from my African principality and come home. Indeed, it was she who, the first time I saw her, urged me to go. I was sitting at the door of my hut; all the others were asleep; the forest was still, except for the distant roaring of a lion. I had been thinking that, my life being so objectless and valueless, I might as well live it in one way as another, and that it would perhaps be best to marry this black princess who had so set her heart upon me, and breed a race of savage kings who should live and rule and die innocent of the triumphs and shames of our civilisation. Then I looked up; and out of the darkest aisle of the tropic wood I saw Hildegarde come towards me. She came quite close to me, with her eyes upon mine ; I was neither amazed nor afraid ; it was as if I had expected her. She raised her right hand, on which was the opal ring I gave her, and pointed to the east. " You must leave this and go, Ralph," she said. " I will tell you the day when you must start, and I will guide you to the sea." I answered that I would be ready ; and she passed to my left round the corner of the hut. As soon as she was gone, the amazement and fear came ; I sprang up to follow her, but I could not find her. For two days I waited, and she did not return. I began to say to myself that I had dreamed. But on the third night I slept ; and in the midst of my sleep I felt a touch on my face, and she was there. I arose and followed her ; we passed through the village ; she showed me my course by the stars, and suddenly I was alone. But I went on till morning ; and if ever I got astray from the path, I fancied I felt a touch directing me aright.   So it was for many days, and I came to trust in her as the sailor trusts to his compass.   Often she warned me of perils that would otherwise have destroyed me.   I gained the coast, as you know, and reached this place by devious routes.   To-night she told me that my journey was not ended yet ; I am still to go eastward, and now in your company.   And yet—all this is insanity!'

'But you are not insane,' I replied ; 'you are not even suffering from monomania. Monomaniacs cannot reason about their infirmity, or perceive that it is abnormal. Your experience cannot be explained on that ground.'

'There is no other explanation, however,' remarked he.

'There are hundreds of thousands of persons who will assure you that the thing is

in accordance with known principles of life,
They will tell you that the spirits of the
dead can revisit those they love, to warn and
guide them. They would regard your case as
a model example of their belief. Why should
not you believe it too?'

'Sooner than accept that theory,' replied
Ralph, 'I prefer the alternative of my own
insanity. The spirits that respond to our
invitations are but the complement of our
own foolish and impious curiosity. They are
the undigested fragments of humanity, swim-
ming in the cosmic stomach, as yet neither
cast irrevocably to waste, nor taken up into
the blood of heaven. Hildegarde is not such
an one; nor, if she were, should I recognise
her, or she me. I was clear on that head
long before this experience began, and I cannot abandon my conviction now, to gratify a
personal longing.'

'Is there nothing in the Buddhistic creed

to meet your want?' I asked. 'Do you put no faith in their analysis of man? Might not this apparition be the astral form of Hildegarde, which her love projects towards you?'

Ralph shook his head. 'I am not competent to judge of the Hindoo philosophy,' he remarked ; 'but even if their scheme has any truth in it, it would not apply to this case. The astral form is the emanation and emissary of a living human being. Hildegarde being dead, has, according to them, passed into the state of Devachan, there to remain until the period of her next incarnation ; and whatever of her so-called fourth principle remains in the astral light, would be incapable of any independent action. But Conrad and I have often discussed the whole subject, and I never could feel any assurance that the entire Buddhistic system is anything more than an ingenious and supple series of inventions to meet each difficulty as it arises.'

Hereupon I felt that if there were ever to be a time when the story of my experiences with Conrad was to be of any avail to Ralph, that time was now come. Accordingly, I began with the mysterious episode at Schandau ; I recounted, in passing, my conversation with Burlace about Catalina's interest in his investigation of disease germs ; and pointed out the sinister light which, in my opinion, it seemed to cast upon Hildegarde's sudden seizure by one of these very diseases. I spoke of Catalina's scarcely disguised acknowledgment of the justice of my suspicions, and her defiant attitude. Then I described Conrad's strange lightsomeness of demeanour, his half-jesting conversation, his invitation to me to visit his study,—and the sight I beheld behind the black curtain.

Ralph had listened, thus far, without a movement or response of any kind, even when I suggested that Hildegarde had been poisoned by her step-mother. He was never wont to be disturbed by the irrevocable. But at this point I perceived a change in the manner of his listening ; his breathing, now held back to hear, and now taken in a quick sigh ; and the slight involuntary shift-ings of his attitude, betrayed how strained was his attention. I went on to portray, as best I could, the extraordinary phantasma-goria that had followed in the pentagonal chamber, culminating in the appearance of Hildegarde herself, in her habit as she lived ; her seeming recognition of me, and how, before she could speak, the hand of death had fastened on her once more.

' I did not know what to think of it then, and I don't know now,' I concluded. ' But since hearing your story, I cannot help think-ing that Conrad may have some explanations to make which it would be worth your while to listen to.'

'Possibly!' murmured Ralph, absently; 'possibly!' Presently he got up and took his hat. 'I must think over this,' he said. 'There may be a chance yet for my sanity. And yet it might be wiser to leave that in doubt, and go no further!'

CHAPTER XII.

TWO MEN.

THE next day but one, Ralph and I were passengers on a steamship of the Bremen line. These steamers stop at Southampton. I left the vessel at that port, and went on by rail to London. Ralph was to continue the voyage to Bremen, and then proceed to Dresden.

I expected to be detained in London a week. After that, I promised Ralph that I would follow him to the Saxon capital. He made a point of this ; he seemed anxious to have a friendly supporter at hand.

On the trip over, we had uniformly avoided the topic that must have been upper-

most in his mind. We conversed on general
matters ; and I noticed that Ralph's character
had mellowed and deepened since the old
Dresden days. His intellectual strength and
mastery were as signal as before, but his
eagerness and love of conflict were gone ; and
he no longer looked forward to the world's
future and his own, as he was used to do.
He seemed more willing to learn than to
teach. He spent much time in reverie. The
masculine sternness of his face was, at such
periods, touchingly softened ; I could read in
its lines something of his experience that he
had never told me ; the thoughts and emotions that had turned his hair gray before its
time. But again, I caught from his eyes a
light of unfulfilled purpose and anticipation.
There was still something for him to do or
suffer—God knew what.

One of the first persons I met in London
was Burlace. He was altered, and for the

worse. His loud, obstreperous voice had become morose and complaining; his face was pale and relaxed; his bearing, instead of being aggressive and brisk, was sullen and lurching; when I saw him he was slouching down the Strand with a short pipe hanging from the corner of his mouth; and I had not heard him speak a dozen words before I surmised that he had been too familiar with gin.

However, he seemed glad to see me, and as anxious to talk as if he had been restricted to his own company for months. I tried to postpone the interview until such time as he should be in a less liquorish humour; but he would not be put off, and dragged me down a side alley to a dingy little inn, where he assured me I could get the best Hollands in town. 'I know the folks here,' he remarked, 'and they keep a special tap for me.' So we had Hollands and birds-eye tobacco and dirt.

And Burlace said, 'Say, old man, here's a c'nundrum. Am I married or single ? '

' You may see double,' I replied, ' but you were made for a bachelor, and you are one.'

' When you said I was made for a bachelor, you did not think I had lived to be married— did you, now ? But married I am, all the same, though it's true I've lived a bachelor ever since.'

' Come,' I said, ' you don't know what you're saying.'

He struck his great paw on the table. ' I am married, I tell you—to Catalina, widow of the late Herman Hertrugge, of Dresden. If you don't believe it, go there and find out. She can't deny it—God damn her ! '

He stared at me with inflamed eyes, and wagged his head.

' Where is your wife ? ' I inquired.

' In Hell, for all I know ; but when I saw her last she was in her drawing-room in Dres-

den.   Look here, old man, you've always been
a friend of mine ; I'll tell you the story.'   I
need not reproduce any further the manner of
his speech ; but his story was strange enough.
He had proposed to Catalina on the day before
Hildegarde's betrothal reception, and she had
agreed to marry him after her step-daughter's
wedding should have taken place, ' if she lives
to be wedded !' she had added, in a jesting
way.   He knew the terms of the will, and understood her to mean that she would marry
him any way.   After Hildegarde's death he
reminded her of her promise, and the day was
fixed.   The wedding was to be a quiet one, in
the bride's house ; Conrad had shown himself
well disposed to the affair, and all looked pros-
perous.   The guests came ; the priest called
the bride and groom before him, and pronounced the words that made them man and
wife.   But no sooner had the final vows been
spoken, than Catalina uttered a terrible shriek,

and fainted. Every one was disconcerted ;
only Conrad retained his presence of mind ; he
explained to the guests that his step-mother
had been labouring under considerable nervous
excitement during several days previous, and
that this was a not unnatural culmination of
her condition. The decks having been thus
cleared, Catalina was taken to her room, and
presently revived. She still manifested unac-
countable agitation ; and when her new husband ventured to propose that they should
get into their carriage and begin their
wedding journey, she trembled so violently
that he feared another fainting fit, and post-
poned the matter until the afternoon. By that
time, Catalina seemed to have recovered her
nerve ; she put on her travelling dress and
came down-stairs, laughing at her late indis-
position, and declaring that she had never felt
better. The carriage was at the kerb ; she
came out leaning on her husband's arm, and

his heart was overflowing with delightful an-
ticipations.   The footman opened the carriage
door, and Catalina's foot was on the step.

There was nothing at all in the carriage
except the cushions ; but Catalina suddenly
stopped and grew as rigid as iron, and the
hand which Burlace held in his became icy
cold.   She made no outcry, but her face
assumed an expression that made even Burlace's lusty blood run cold.   Her lips parted,
and she seemed to gasp for air ; then a tremor
shook her from head to foot, and she fell back
in her husband's arms.   He thought she had
died of a stroke of the heart, and, with the
assistance of the footman, carried her back
into the house.   He and Conrad worked over
her for an hour, and at last succeeded in bringing her back to consciousness.   But now her
courage and self-control seemed utterly broken
down ; she was as weak and garrulous as an
invalid child ; she exhibited terror whenever

Burlace approached her, and shuddered when he addressed her. She either could or would not give any explanation of her state. Evening came on, and it was necessary to give up all idea of starting on their trip that day. Catalina remained in her room in charge of a nurse, and Burlace, refusing Conrad's offer of a cot-bed in the library, went to an hotel and spent his wedding night there.

The next morning he presented himself at the house, and was told that his wife would see him. He went to her room, and found her propped up with pillows on her bed. She was alone, and signed to him to sit down. He drew up a chair, but she begged him in a nervous tone not to sit so near.

She told him that she could never live with him as his wife. She evaded giving any definite or comprehensible reason for this decision, but said that any attempt to fulfil her marriage duties would, she was well con-

vinced, result in her death. He pressed her
energetically to be more explicit ; she became
pitifully agitated, and the words that fell from
her seemed to mean, if they meant anything,
that she fancied herself to have committed some
hideous crime, and that she had received a
warning from the grave. He expostulated,
entreated, even stormed and raged, in vain.
He swore that he would take her with him by
force, at which she burst into an hysteric
laugh, and asked him if he were stronger than
death ?   Later, she offered to make any arrangement as regarded money matters that he
chose to suggest, even to surrendering three-
fourths of her fortune ; but with this Burlace
would have nothing to do. He would have
her or nothing. He left her at last, she being
in a condition of semi-collapse, and he in a frame
of mind half way between the murderous and
the suicidal.   He rambled about the streets
all day and night ; the morning following he

came back to the house, determined to enforce his rights.

He was met by Conrad, who told him that Catalina had left Dresden. He said that he believed her mind was affected; that she appeared to imagine she was haunted or pursued by a malignant spirit. 'So far as I can make out,' Conrad had added, 'she has got a notion that she was somehow instrumental in bringing about the death of my sister Hildegarde, and she goes so far as to allude to you as if you were her accomplice in the affair. It is ridiculous, of course; and her adhering to it is evidence of her mental unsoundness.' Conrad had gone on to say that Catalina had extracted a promise from him not to reveal to Burlace the place of her retreat; but he held out hopes that she would, if allowed to remain in quiet for awhile, regain her equipoise, and that their married felicity would then resume an uninterrupted course. Burlace, utterly worn out in brain and body, was unable to struggle any longer ; he gave Conrad an address where to write to him in case of any favourable change ; then he threw himself into a train and came to London.

'And I've been here ever since,' he added, emptying his fourth glass of Hollands, and staring sullenly at the dregs in the bottom. 'But I understand the whole damned swindle now. She was in love with that fellow Ralph Merlin, and she is scheming to get him. It's all very clever and cunning. Maybe she did murder Hildegarde ; I remember she came one day to look through my microscope ; and there was some stuff about that would have poisoned half Dresden, and no one the wiser. The girl was in her way, and it would be natural enough. I don't know where Ralph is ; but if ever I find that he has been within reach of her I'll squeeze the life out of her white throat with these fingers of mine !' He

held them up before me, in his sullen, drunken
rage. ' But all that about her being haunted,
and her fainting and shrieking,—that was all
lies and humbug. They had made a fool of me
between 'em ; but the end has not come yet.
Look here ! do you know where Ralph is ? '

He thrust his face abruptly into mine as
he asked the question, as if he were ready to
suspect me of being in the ' plot' against him.
Although I did not attach much weight to his
maunderings, and was rather disposed to
think that a dose of Ralph might prove a good
thing for him, I prevaricated to the extent of
reminding him that Ralph's death had been
reported a year ago, and that if he had returned to life since, I had seen no mention of
it in the newspapers. But Burlace had by
this time lost the faculty of holding a conse-
cutive train of thought ; he diverged on one
topic after another, and finally broke into
sobs, and called me to witness how he wor-

shipped Catalina. 'I don't care what she did,' he cried, sticking his big knuckles in his eyes, like a schoolboy; 'if she had cut the girl's throat with a carving-knife, I'd have married her just as quick. I love her; and when that's said, everything's said—isn't it? She might be as wicked as she likes. What's wickedness, what's morality, I'd like to know? Do you remember my thermometer? I believe in nothing; you know that; not in God, nor Devil. But I loved that woman as no one else ever loved her, or ever will. She'll find it out some day. I'd have stood by her in anything, no matter what—good or bad. I'm a good fellow, too,—or I was, before this happened. I'm a drunkard and a good-for-nothing loafer now; I know that as well as you do; and she did it. Well, that's all right. Have some more gin? Where are you stopping here?'

I gave him my address, not expecting him

to remember it, and soon after left him. What he had said of himself was true; he was a man of good natural abilities, and no mean accomplishments. But he believed in nothing; and therefore a woman had been able to ruin him.

A few days later I received a letter from Ralph, with the Dresden post-mark. ' Come here as soon as you can leave your business,' he wrote. ' I have seen Conrad; in fact, he met me at the train, and seemed to have known I was coming. You know his foible is to seem to know everything beforehand; and certainly he has queer gifts. I have told him nothing of my experience; but some things he has said appear to indicate that he is somehow cognisant of it. I believe Catalina is in Dresden, or not far away from it; I have not seen her, and don't suppose I shall. Conrad tells me she was married to Burlace, but has never lived with him; I don't know the reason of either fact. Next week, Conrad intends to have some sort of a reception at his house. I have a notion that this occasion will have an especial significance for me ; and I want you to be present.' After alluding to some other subjects, he said, ' I have had no visions since arriving here ; but nevertheless there has been a constant sense of Hildegarde's proximity. I feel as if I should learn more about her soon ; and yet I feel as if it might be best, both for her and for me, if I left Dresden at once and for ever. But if so, I lack the resolution to act upon the impression. I shall see the matter to its end, let it issue how it will. And I depend on you.'

I arrived in Dresden on the morning of the day of Conrad's proposed reception. I was driven to the Hotel Bellevue ; but finding it full, I told the *kutscher* to take me to the Hotel de Saxe. There, somewhat to my perplexity, I found rooms already engaged for me, and a note from Conrad, asking me to give him the pleasure of my company that evening.

CHAPTER XIII.

AN EXPERIMENT.

THE time appointed for me to present myself at Conrad's was an hour or so earlier than for the other guests ; and when I entered I found only him and Ralph. I had met the latter earlier in the day. Conrad greeted me with much cordiality.

' Ralph and I have been at our old work,' he said, laughing ; ' we have resumed our duel in the realms of the transcendental. My conviction is that life has a much closer relation to the body than extremists on the other side are willing to admit. The body, we are agreed, is the direct creation of the soul, and only indirectly that of God—I am availing myself of

my opponent's terminology—whose proper
activity begins and ends with the soul only.
God produces only what is, namely, man the
spirit; and His creative attitude towards this
spirit results in what appears to be, namely,
the body of man, and the rest of the material
universe. Now, my point is this :—what we
call the mortal life of a person is the persist-
ence, for a certain period in the case of that
person, of this result of a creative attitude
which is permanent as regards mankind at
large. In other words, though man is constantly incarnate, individual human beings
are constantly disincarnating, or, as we say,
dying. The question then arises, what is the
cause of this individual disincarnation, and
can it be arrested?'

'Individuals die, because individuals are
born,' said Ralph 'Mankind does not die,
because there was never a time when it did
not exist.'

'Conceding that for the moment,' returned Conrad, ' the more practical problem remains, can death be arrested? If the body only seems to be, at best, why may not that seeming be indefinitely prolonged? Is it not true that death is, essentially, a change in the soul, —the arrival of a moment when one phase of its activity terminates, and another phase begins? Evidently, then, if we wish to postpone death, we must direct our efforts first to the soul. We must devise some means by which the soul can be induced or compelled to delay entering upon its second phase, and to continue in its first or physical one. Are you bold enough to affirm that such a fact is beyond the skill of human science?'

' Suppose the body to have been blown to atoms by an explosion,' I began; but he interrupted me with a laugh.

'I admit technical difficulties in such a case,' said he; ' though less, perhaps, as re-

gards the physical than the spiritual predica-
ment ; for do not our friends, the spiritualists,
tell us tales about "materialising" spirits ?
But take the case that the body, at the moment of the change, is substantially sound,
though (let us say) it has been attacked by a
fatal disease,—or, to speak more philosophic-
ally, the soul has suffered from certain delusions which are reflected on the physical plane
as derangement of bodily function, or disin-
tegration of tissue. My contention would be
that the correction of this delusion would
restore the soul (and, as a corollary, the body)
to a normal state, and re-establish physical
life.'

'Well,' said Ralph—and he threw a peculiar glance at me as he spoke—'that seems to
be a sufficiently ingenious theory. Have you
any practical illustrations to adduce in
support of it ? '

'It is hardly fair to tempt me to discredit

P

my good logic with imperfect facts,' returned Conrad, laughing again ; ' but are you really desirous to push the matter to a test? '

' To be frank with you,' Ralph rejoined, ' I do desire it, and I do not. If such a thing as you propose can be done, I hold it to be a profanation of the most unmitigated sort,— the black art in its worst form. At the same time, I am weak enough to put you to the proof ; if you can do it, let it be done.'

' Your invitation might be more cordial,' remarked Conrad, lightly. ' As to the black art, my dear Ralph, you know it is not at all in my line. My investigations, such as they are, have been strictly on the lines laid down by Nature. I am only a beginner in science ; but I think I have one advantage over scientific men in general, in that I recognise and make my account with both sides of Nature, instead of with the physical side exclusively. Study of the one throws light upon the other, and speculations on the spirit suggest experiments on the body. But you shall judge for yourself; and, by the way, I have a right to expect indulgence in this case, from you especially. Step into my study.'

He led the way, and we followed. The pentagonal chamber looked much as it did when I had seen it last; but now a handsome antique chest of carved oak rested upon the iron pentagon beneath the great magnet. It was secured by three massive locks.

'This chest,' observed Conrad, 'has not been opened since I closed it nearly two years ago. You have only my word for this; but I will say that I have no object in deceiving you. Here are the keys,' he added, taking them from a hook on the wall; 'will you oblige me, Ralph, by unlocking the thing, and lifting the lid?'

Ralph hesitated a moment, as if summoning his resolution. Then he took the keys from Conrad's hand, and turned them, one after the other, in the locks. After another pause, he grasped the edges of the lid with both hands, and flung it back with such violence that it was torn from its hinges, and fell with a crash to the floor. A powerful aromatic odour immediately filled the room.

The coffer was filled to the brim with some substance resembling amber, in pieces about the size of a raisin. It was from this, apparently, that the pleasant odour emanated. But what struck me particularly was the fact that this odour. though much stronger, was the same that I had noticed in my room in New York, at the time when Ralph was visited by the vision of Hildegarde ; and I perceived that Ralph recognised it also, and his face flushed red. He looked at Conrad with a sort of fierceness.

'What is this ?' he demanded. 'Play me no tricks.'

'It's merely a variety of aromatic gum,' returned Conrad, in a matter-of-fact tone, 'which I placed here on account of its purifying and preservative qualities. It lies,' as you see, in a shallow tray, and can be removed without trouble.' He suited the action to the word, lifting out the tray, which he laid to one side. The space beneath appeared to be closely packed with folded cloths, of the texture of fine lawn, and having a pale, yellow hue, probably due to some solution in which they had been steeped. As Ralph remained motionless, Conrad proceeded to remove these cloths one by one, until he had uncovered a long object, of roughly cylindrical shape, swathed in a covering of heavy linen, sewn up lengthwise down the centre. Its outlines conveyed the suggestion of the human form.

'Have either of you a pen-knife?' inquired Conrad. 'We shall have to rip open this covering in order to come at what is inside.'

Ralph still made no sign. I took my knife from my pocket, and, at a nod from Conrad, cut the thread of the seam from end to end. The covering fell apart.

There was a filling of dried rose leaves within ; but these sifted down on either side, and revealed—what, of course, I had all along expected to see—the pure, pale countenance of Hildegarde.

'What do you think ?' said Conrad, appealing to me, as a sculptor might ask my opinion of his statue. 'I can see no change ; can you ?'

'None !' said I.

'And, indeed, after the lapse of these two years, she seemed as fresh and untouched as on the day when she stood beside Ralph as his betrothed wife. The skin seemed soft and pliant ; the long eyelashes, resting on the cheeks, needed but a thought to lift them ; and the curved line between the lips would melt at a breath. And yet, for two years, no breath had passed them, nor had any light visited the eyes.

'What say you, my friend ?' asked Conrad, regarding Ralph curiously.

'It is a wonderful piece of work,' he returned, in a measured voice. 'Not so warm as a painting, nor so ideal as sculpture ; but the Egyptians themselves could not have done better. Of what use is it ?'

'Her soul might find a use for it,' remarked the other, with a smile.

'What God has parted cannot be reunited,' said Ralph, coldly.

'But you loved her, did you not ? and love, if all reports be true, is stronger than death. Will you test the proverb ?'

'No ; not even if I knew that love could work the miracle. She and I will meet hereafter ; but I should not deserve her love, if, for the sake of comforting my few years of earth, I called her back from heaven.'

These words were spoken in a low voice, weighted with emotion ; and as he spoke, he turned away.

Conrad shrugged his shoulders. ' That is well said, Ralph,' he observed ; ' but, after all, you are moralising over what you believe to be an impossibility. If you were convinced that she would rise up at your word, like Lazarus in the New Testament, I fancy the word would not be wanting. Well, then, since love refuses, let us see what science can do ! I have more faith than you, though this is an experiment based, hitherto, upon theory alone.'

He stepped to the upper corner of the room and touched a small disk embedded there ; and immediately there followed a gentle whispering sound which I dimly remembered, and the great magnet began to discharge its vital energy. The invisible current swept downwards on the peaceful face beneath it; and we, who stood apart, felt something of the exhilarating coolness. The dried leaves of the roses that were heaped along the sides of the figure were stirred; and it seemed to me that some of them lost their dryness, and that their original softness and colour came back to them.

Conrad kept his strange eyes rivetted on the face in the coffer with an intensity of gaze that almost seemed to emit a visible ray. Ralph's eyes were downcast, and partly averted; but he was evidently struggling against a terrible attraction; the tender, human instincts of his nature were fighting against the barrier of principle and reason. Time both flies and stands still at such junctures; the great magnet vibrated; and now it was beyond doubt that some of the petals of the roses were as fresh as when first shaken from the stem. But the peaceful face was peaceful and unresponsive still.

Those moments of suspense were exhausting, even to me, who was but an onlooker. The possibility that hung in the balance was of such gigantic significance—the very meaning of human existence seeming to hinge upon it—that the mind shrank from contemplating it. And now that the experiment had gone so far, success and failure appeared alike terrible.

Suddenly, Conrad raised both his arms, with the hands open and prone, and brought them downwards, and then again upwards, with a slow, sweeping movement. He was standing near the foot of the coffer, so that the gesture was as if he had caught some invisible substance in the air, and driven it over the dead girl, from her feet to her head. He repeated this gesture three times ; and at the same moment the discharge from the magnet ceased, the rushing sound was heard no more, and the chamber became as still as an Egyptian tomb in the heart of a hill.

Conrad's arms fell to his sides ; he shivered, and a grayish pallor crept over his features, in which appeared lines that made him look like an old man. The experiment, then, had failed.

Ralph raised his head and looked sternly and scornfully at him. ' You yourself deserve to die,' he said ; ' but you have dragged me into your own humiliation, and I am not worthy to inflict your punishment.'

Conrad cast a haggard glance at the corpse.

' I would gladly have died to succeed,' he muttered.

' Be thankful that you did not succeed ; what are you, or any man, to turn law into chaos, and gain a victory over Nature ! '

But, all in an instant, an electric shock seemed to run through Conrad, and set his soul on fire. An awful ecstasy of triumph glared out of his face. His hair bristled on his head, and he gnashed his teeth together.

'See! see!' he shrieked, tossing his arms aloft and stamping his feet on the floor. 'I have not failed! She lives! she lives! Ha! ha! ha! Ralph—Ralph Merlin? Whose is the victory now?'

Ralph stepped forward, and bent a long look into the coffer. Then he grasped Conrad with hands of iron.

'Hush! hush!' he said, in a deep voice. 'If God has permitted this thing, let us meet it with reverence; it may mean the greatest blessing, or the greatest curse, of time!'

And even as he spoke, Hildegarde opened her eyes, and sat erect. She seemed perplexed; but, meeting Ralph's eyes, she smiled as if reassured.

CHAPTER XIV.

ON ONE CONDITION.

THE emotion of wonder is one of the most vehement of all; and it is also one of the most transitory. Imagination revels in it, but the mind cannot tolerate it; and no sooner has a marvel taken place, than we compel it, willy-nilly, into some sort of accordance with the routine of experience. If we could not do this, we should probably lose our reason altogether. Nature abhors not a vacuum more than does human nature a miracle.

That first sharp stab of amazement, when my eyes saw her who had lain dead for two years return to life, lasted but a few blind moments. It took but those few moments for me to raise and readjust my whole conception of law and order. Law and order still existed, and were as immutable as ever; it was my view of them that had changed. By the time Hildegarde had gained her feet, and had uttered the first few words of her new life, I had accommodated myself to the situation, and nothing remained but the agreeable excitement of an interesting novelty.

Of course, other elements entered into the emotions of Ralph and Conrad, to whom the event was quite as much personal as general in its bearings. But it was at once perceived by all of us that Hildegarde must be introduced only by the most circumspect degrees to the knowledge of what had befallen her; and for a while we were sufficiently occupied in parrying her questions and managing her curiosity. She remembered having been taken suddenly ill; she recalled a darkened room

and the hushed voice of nurses ; and the last
circumstance in her recollection was of Conrad's saying to her, 'Now, I will put you to
sleep.' He had several times exercised this
power over her, and she had soon felt herself
succumbing to the influence. The rest was a
blank. But how had she got into that box ?
what were the rose-leaves there for ? and
how happened it that Ralph, in the space of a
few hours, had contrived to grow a beard and
to get gray hairs ? These things required explanation ; and who was to explain them ?

'That was a good sleep you gave me,
Conrad,' she remarked. 'I was very ill
before ; I thought I might be going to die ;
but now I am better and stronger than I ever
was ; and all in such a little while ! '

What is a little while ? What a thing
time is, to be sure !

It was moving to observe Ralph's profound
preoccupation with her,—his tremulous, almost

speechless emotion,—and her happy unconsciousness of anything stranger than his beard.
No shadow remained on her mind of the great
gulf which she had crossed, and crossed again.
She had brought with her no tidings of the
other world ; and yet she had been there, and
had experienced what no other human being
had done.

Conrad had drawn Ralph aside, and conversed with him a few minutes ; and then he
beckoned to me, and I followed him out of the
room.

'We may as well leave the lovers to
explain themselves to each other,' he said.
He had quite recovered from the wild burst of
excitement with which he had greeted the
success of his experiment, just when all had
seemed to be lost. 'I may as well tell you,'
he went on, 'that I have made all arrangements to have them married this evening.
There are several reasons for this, and at all

events their betrothal has lasted quite
long enough. The guests will be here in
a few minutes. To avoid complications, I
have invited only such persons as are unac-
quainted with the peculiar circumstances,
and have heard nothing of my sister's reputed
death.'

' Did she die, indeed ? ' I asked.

' Really, my dear fellow, I can hardly tell
you. According to all precedent she did.
But you shall hear just how the matter
stands. Catalina, as you have no doubt surmised, under cover of scientific curiosity,
visited Burlace in his laboratory, and secured
some of the microscopic germs that he was
investigating. Nothing is easier than to ad-
minister these germs in the food or drink ;
and neither the victim nor the physician can
prove that a crime has been committed ; a
disease has established itself, and it runs its
course, which, in this instance, was bound to

Q

be fatal; but there is no trace of murder outside the mind of the murderer.

'After making trial of all recognised means of combating the disease, I saw that the girl must die. Then I resolved to put to the test a theory which I had speculated upon long before. I waited until she was almost in the act of death; another ten minutes would have seen the end. I had magnetised her several times previously, both to relieve small ailments to which she was occasionally subject, and also, now and then, for certain purposes of my own. Therefore, she was completely under what is called my magnetic control. I put forth the influence, and though there was more resistance on her part than I had expected to find, she yielded at last, and fell into the trance.

'I argued that as long as she remained in this condition—which, to one unfamiliar with its peculiar symptoms, is indistinguishable from death—the action of the poison on her system would be arrested. And not only might it be arrested ; it might, after a certain lapse of time, disappear altogether, the germs themselves becoming devoid of life. As to this last, however, I was probably mistaken. My subsequent study of the germs tends to show that they are practically indestructible, once they have got a lodgment in the body. But be that as it may, I was perfectly successful in the other matter. The progress of the disease stopped short at the instant she fell into the trance ; and it has remained inactive from that day to this.'

'You have kept her in a trance for two years ?'

'Certainly ; and she might have continued so indefinitely. Meanwhile, she was pronounced dead ; her body was put in the coffin, and her funeral was duly solemnised. A few weeks later, without attracting any attention, I had her conveyed to my rooms, and placed her in the coffer where you saw her to-day. She has lain there ever since. You saw what occurred this evening. And that, in brief, is the history of the case.'

It was a strange history ; but it seemed to me that the strangest features of it had been omitted, and that Conrad was designedly slurring over these features. What about the apparition that I had seen emerge from behind the black curtain in the pentagonal chamber?

And what of those visitations which had guided Ralph from the centre of Africa round the world? Nor was I by any means satisfied that an ordinary trance would present the same characteristics as this of Hildegarde's. The body would dry up and perish in much less time than two years.

When I questioned Conrad on these points, he answered somewhat evasively.

' The phenomena you speak of were pro-

bably entirely imaginary,' he said. 'At all
events, how can there be any connection
between them and the experiment I was
describing?'

'I don't know what the connection is, but
there is one; and I believe that it was of
your making. I have not forgotten
Schandau.'

'You must bear in mind that very little
is understood of the real nature of trance,' he
finally remarked. 'The body is wholly
quiescent, but the spirit and the principles
intermediate between that and the body may
possess a greater freedom and activity than
before. Nothing would, be dispersed or
dissipated, as is the case in actual death; but
a being would exist in the astral light, pos-
sessing some qualities nearly allied to the
physical, and yet capable of passing from
place to place with the rapidity and docility
of thought. Now, there seems to be a special

relation between the trance-being and the will or thoughts of the magnetiser. Possibly it retains no will of its own, or but little. In that case it would be in a measure subject to the will and thought of the magnetiser, when strongly concentrated and exerted, and would be present in any place on which his attention was fixed. But really, the whole question is so obscure that I am perplexed about it myself. As to the condition of the body after so long a lapse of time, I may fairly take some credit to myself for it,' he added, with a smile. 'That affair of the magnet and pentagon is an invention, or at least an adaptation, of my own. Some elements enter into its construction that do not appear on the surface ; and you have felt as well as seen something of its powers. Of course, it was not that that restored Hildegarde to life,—or, if you prefer it, roused her from her trance. Its effect was physical merely ; it refreshed

the body, and prepared it for its inhabitant.
It was by reversing the passes that had en-
tranced her, that I succeeded in bringing
her round,—though I confess there was a
moment when I felt a trifle uneasy over the
result.'

' I fancied you looked a little bit put out
just then ; though I thought you seemed
pleased just afterwards. But there is one
thing about this business, Conrad,' I added,
dropping the ironic vein, ' that seems to me
to counterbalance all you have gained. The
germs of the poison, you say, cannot be destroyed. If that be so, Hildegarde has only
a reprieve: The return of life will be to her
but a return of death, and the more tragic
because it is a return. In how many days, or
hours, this will come to pass, you probably
know better than I ; but if you have not
provided against it, I don't know why you
are not a worse murderer than Catalina.'

'I have had it under consideration constantly almost since the first,' he returned, rather gloomily; 'and though I have not quite cleared up the difficulty, yet I have at least ensured the prolongation of Hildegarde's life indefinitely,—provided that she observes certain easy conditions.'

' What are they ? '

' They involve only her remaining always within a few hours' journey of this place. The poison in her system is not likely to be quiescent more than two or three days ; and as soon as it begins to act, she must again be thrown into the trance, and afterwards subjected to the influence of the great magnet. This treatment is indispensable, and it will probably have to be repeated at regular intervals. But the annoyance is slight, and, in view of the result, I don't imagine that either she or Ralph will object. And now,' he broke off, 'our guests are beginning to

arrive. The clergyman will be here immediately, and I must prepare the lovers for the
happiness in store for them.'

He went out, and left me to my meditations, which were not of an entirely roseate
hue. I had acquired the impression that
Conrad had some ulterior end in view in all
this, which was not of a wholly unselfish
character, andi t seemed to me that the necessity of constantly renewing Hildegarde's vitality, and of subjecting her at such short intervals to the absolute control of her brother,
might prove more irksome than he seemed
to anticipate. But I tried to hope for the
best.

In the drawing-room several persons were
already assembled. I had met none of them
before, and it was evident that they had been
summoned chiefly to act as witnesses of what
was about to take place. Conrad entered,
escorting the clergyman, a youngish man,

with an amiable and feeble face. A lawyer was also in attendance to oversee the preparation and signing of the marriage contract. Finally, Ralph came in, with Hildegarde on his arm.

I presume that Hildegarde had by this time been made acquainted with the facts of her condition. Her face, always extremely sensitive in reflecting the states of her spirit, wore an expression of wistful solemnity, tempered with the tenderness of an exalted love, that somehow brought tears to my eyes. Ralph, on the other hand, had a look about him that was quite new to me, and that I did not altogether like. The colour in his face was warm, and his eyes lively and bright; a smile hovered constantly about his mouth, and he kept looking at Hildegarde with glances that were not merely lover-like, but idolatrous, and even seemed to express a sensuousness of feeling that was out of keeping

with my friend's depth and gravity of character. He rather avoided my eye, and when
I congratulated him, he said, ' We owe
everything to Conrad. Science and humanity
ought to unite in canonising that man. I
can never excuse myself for the way in which
I spoke to him to-day. But I see the error
of my way, and am not likely to make such
an ass of myself again. Is not the mere flesh
and blood of such a woman as that worth a
thousand souls? '

' Is she immortal? ' returned I.

' What is immortality? ' said he, with a
short laugh. ' We know what is, but who
can tell what may be ? '

The clergyman advanced ; the couple took
their places beside each other ; the guests
gathered round, and the words of the covenant
were uttered. Conrad stood behind the bride,
and as the ceremony ended, his figure seemed
to grow taller and dilate, as if some long-de-

sired triumph had at last been won. What was the meaning of it?

The papers remained to be signed. Ralph wrote his name first. Then Hildegarde took the pen in her hand. As she laid it down again, having affixed her signature, the door at the end of the room opened, and Catalina entered.

CHAPTER XV.

MARRIAGE.

HER appearance was entirely unexpected by everybody save Conrad ; his face at once took on an expression of malicious satisfaction. And in a moment I realised the whole significance of the event. He had inflicted upon this woman a revenge as ingenious as it was overwhelming.

Having first convinced her of Hildegarde's death, at the same time leading her to suppose that he was wholly unsuspicious of her agency in it, he had put her in a position where she fancied herself free to marry without prejudice to the terms of her husband's will. The motives that induced her to yield to Burlace's

suit, though love could scarcely have been one
of them, were still urgent enough to make the
act comprehensible.   But it was not a part of
Conrad's scheme to permit her to profit by
Burlace's protection.   Whether he had any
hand in the mysterious occurrences that kept
them apart, and what, precisely, those occurrences were, you can probably conjecture as
easily as I.

But Hildegarde was not dead; she was
alive; and she was not separated for ever from
Ralph ; she was his wife.   Therefore, not
only was Catalina deprived of her fortune and
thrown helpless on the world, but she was
compelled to behold her rival's triumph and
felicity, which she had staked and lost her
own salvation to prevent.

She did not at first see Hildegarde, and
Conrad immediately stepped forward to greet
her with a great manifestation of cordiality.
He held her in conversation for a few minutes,

and then led her up the room, saying, in a voice that all might hear :

' Ralph, and Mrs. Merlin, our celebration would have been incomplete if my step-mother had not kindly consented to come and offer you her congratulations.'

Catalina stopped short, as if she had run against a wall in the dark. Her black eyes wavered for a moment, but finally fixed themselves upon Hildegarde in a ghastly stare. Then, with her hands outstretched, she drew nearer, step by step. Her face, though beautiful still, was awful to look upon at that crisis. She had not passed unscathed through these two years ; there were lines around her mouth and beneath her eyes that suggested tortured nerves, and vain attempts to drug them into insensibility. And these traces were dreadfully emphasised by the emotion of the juncture.

She crept toward her rival as if controlled

by a mixture of terror and desperate curiosity. At length, when within arm's reach, she doubtfully extended one hand, until the trembling finger-tips came in contact with Hildegarde's shoulder. Probably she had imagined that the girl was but a spectre, and would vanish at a touch. Had Conrad, then, made this innocent spirit the helpless instrument of his malignity?

But when Catalina realised that here was no spectral illusion, but actual flesh and blood, she emitted a sharp breathing sound from her throat, and fell back a step, pressing her hands against her temples. Her eyes rolled in their sockets. After standing so for a while, she began to laugh softly. Oh, surely the cruelest vengeance might have been sated by that piteous spectacle! The shock and bewilderment had been too great for her already failing nerves, and she was going mad before our eyes.

The deep absorption of this episode had kept our attention from a confused noise outside the door. But now the door was flung open, and a heavily-built man, hatless, with disordered dress and flushed face, half staggered and half stalked into the room. It was Will Burlace, savage with drink, and with a passion smouldering in his bloodshot eyes that was not due to drink alone. How had he come there? He must have followed me secretly from London, his morbid suspicions having suggested some new plot on foot against him. His glance singled out Catalina at once, and Ralph standing near her ; and it was plain that he deemed his suspicions fully justified.

'I knew where I should find you, and how I should find you,' he said, as he came towards his wife. 'You thought you could pull the wool over my eyes, but I'm not

R

such a fool. I'll settle with you now. You wouldn't give an honest man your heart, but I'll cut it out of your white body, my dear !'

It was doing Ralph injustice ; but so it was, that he was the last man whom I expected to see step forward to protect Catalina. And yet he was the only one who would. Burlace had a knife in his hand. Catalina lacked either the intelligence or the will to try to escape. Ralph caught the wrist of Burlace's right hand, which held the knife ; and instantly they were engaged in a desperate struggle.

It recalled to my memory that tussle of theirs, years ago ; but that was in play, and this was deadly earnest. Burlace, besides his superior weight, had the fury of his jealous and murderous rage to enforce him ; Ralph seemed to me somewhat less quick and supple than of yore, and twice or thrice I saw him wince, as if from a sharp pain. I had forgot the assegai wound that he had received in Africa.

Burlace bore him back, and I thought he was overcome. But, by a feint, Ralph threw him off his balance ; and then, in a flash, the knife flew from the other's hand ; the two whirled round, and came to the floor with a crash that shook the room. Burlace was undermost, and he lay stunned. Ralph rose, but painfully, with a pallid face, and pressing his hand against his side. His old wound had opened, and he was bleeding internally.

.   .   .   .   .

He lay in great suffering all that night ; and the next morning it was evident that he must die. Hildegarde did not leave him, and it seemed to me that as his strength failed, she also drooped and faded. She looked thin and frail, and her flesh was almost transparent. But the love in her eyes glowed stronger than ever, and instead of grief, she appeared to be inspired with an inward spiritual joy.

Conrad had been observing her critically; and at length he told Ralph plainly that the old poison had already recommenced its fatal work on her, and that it would be necessary to apply the remedy without delay. Ralph took her hand in his, and regarded her steadily. 'You hear what your brother says?' he said.

'All is well with us,' she replied; 'I want no change.'

'But your life depends upon it, Hildegarde.'

'No—not my life,' answered she.

'All that I have done has been for you, Hildegarde!' Conrad exclaimed. 'I have loved you, I have avenged you, I have brought you back to life. Will you leave me now, and render it all vain?'

'I must stay with my husband,' was her reply.

'Let it be so, Conrad,' said Ralph, at last. 'For my part, I am well content with this conclusion. It was all wrong—what you attempted, and I acquiesced in. Had I lived I should have lowered myself, and perhaps her also. There is a wisdom and kindness greater than any we know of. Our little efforts to gain power and wield it—what do they amount to, after all ? The worst grief that nature brings us is not very grievous ; but we have no mercy on ourselves.'

'You are a fool !' said Conrad sullenly, turning away.

Ralph and Hildegarde both died that night. The bodies were put in coffins, and left in the pentagonal chamber. But when the bearers went to remove them, it was found that Hildegarde's coffin contained only a few handfuls of fragrant white dust. At first, I suspected Conrad of some subtle practice, but I have since come to the conclusion that this was a mistake. When Hildegarde's soul left her body for its final flight, nothing remained that could know corruption. And, perhaps, during her long trance, influences had been at work which rendered her apparent recovery little more than a sort of mirage of physical existence, destined to endure but for a moment and then vanish for ever.

But does she not live still, and Ralph with her ? I would rather trust her faith on that point than take my cue from Conrad, though he is now one of the leaders of European science.

PRINTED BY
SPOTTISWOODE AND CO., NEW-STREET SQUARE
LONDON

Besant (Walter), Novels by:
Crown 8vo, cloth extra, 3s. 6d. each ; post 8vo, illust. boards, 2s. each; cloth limp, 2s. 6d. each.

All Sorts and Conditions of Men: An Impossible Story. With Illustrations by FRED. BARNARD.

The Captains' Room, &c. With Frontispiece by E. J. WHEELER.

All In a Garden Fair. With 6 Illustrations by HARRY FURNISS.

Dorothy Forster. With Frontispiece by CHARLES GREEN.

Uncle Jack, and other Stories.

Children of Gibeon.

Crown 8vo, cloth extra, 3s. 6d. each.
The World Went Very Well Then. With Illustrations by A. FORESTIER.
Herr Paulus: His Rise, his Greatness, and his Fall.

EDITION DE LUXE OF A FRENCH CLASSIC.

Abbé Constantin (The). By LUDOVIC HALEVY, of the French Academy. Translated into English. With 36 Photogravure Illustrations by GOUPIL & Co., after the Drawings of Madame MADELEINE LEMAIRE. Only 250 copies of this choice book have been printed (in large quarto) for the English market, each one numbered. The price may be learned from any Bookseller.

About.—The Fellah : An Egyptian Novel. By EDMOND ABOUT. Translated by Sir RANDAL ROBERTS. Post 8vo, illustrated boards, 2s. ; cloth limp, 2s. 6d.

Adams (W. Davenport), Works by:
A Dictionary of the Drama. Being a comprehensive Guide to the Plays, Playwrights, Players, and Playhouses of the United Kingdom and America, from the Earliest to the Present Times. Crown 8vo, half-bound, 12s. 6d. *[Preparing.*
Quips and Quiddities. Selected by W. DAVENPORT ADAMS. Post 8vo, cloth limp, 2s. 6d.

Advertising, A History of, from the Earliest Times. Illustrated by Anecdotes, Curious Specimens, and Notices of Successful Advertisers. By HENRY SAMPSON. With Coloured Frontispiece and Illustrations. Crown 8vo, cloth gilt, 7s. 6d.

Agony Column (The) of "The Times," from 1800 to 1870. Edited, with an Introduction, by ALICE CLAY. Post 8vo, cloth limp, 2s. 6d.

Birthday Books :—
The Starry Heavens: A Poetical Birthday Book. Square 8vo, handsomely bound in cloth, 2s. 6d.
The Lowell Birthday Book. With Illusts. Small 8vo, cloth extra, 4s. 6d.

Blackburn's (Henry) Art Handbooks. Demy 8vo, Illustrated, uniform in size for binding.
Academy Notes, separate years, from 1876 to 1887, each 1s.
Academy Notes, 1888. With numerous Illustrations. 1s.
Academy Notes, 1880-84 Complete in One Volume, with about 700 Facsimile Illustrations. Cloth limp, 6s.
Grosvenor Notes, 1877. 6d.
Grosvenor Notes, separate years, from 1878 to 1887, each 1s.
Grosvenor Notes, 1888. With numerous Illusts. 1s.
Grosvenor Notes, Vol. I., 1877-82.

Aldé (Hamilton), Works by :
Post 8vo, illustrated boards, 2s. each.
Carr of Carrlyon. | Confidences.

Alexander (Mrs.), Novels by :
Post 8vo, illustrated boards, 2s. each.
Maid, Wife, or Widow?
Valerie's Fate.

Allen (Grant), Works by :
Crown 8vo, cloth extra, 6s. each.
The Evolutionist at Large. Second Edition, revised.
Vignettes from Nature.
Colin Clout's Calendar.

Crown 8vo, cloth extra, 6s. each ; post 8vo, illustrated boards., 2s. each.
Strange Stories. With a Frontispiece by GEORGE DU MAURIER.
The Beckoning Hand. With a Frontispiece by TOWNLEY GREEN.

Post 8vo, illustrated boards, 2s. each.
Babylon : A Romance.
In all Shades.

Crown 8vo, cloth extra, 3s. 6d. each.
For Maimie's Sake: A Tale of Love and Dynamite.
The Devil's Die. *[Shortly.*

Philistia. Crown 8vo, cloth extra, 3s. 6d. ; post 8vo, illust. boards, 2s.
This Mortal Coil. Three Vols., crown 8vo.

Architectural Styles, A Handbook of. Translated from the German of A. ROSENGARTEN, by W. COLLETT-SANDARS. Crown 8vo, cloth extra, with 639 Illustrations, 7s. 6d.

Arnold.—Bird Life in England. By EDWIN LESTER ARNOLD. Crown 8vo, cloth extra, 6s.

...teenth Century. With nearly 400 Illustrations, engraved in facsimile of the originals.

Social Life In the Reign of Queen Anne. From Original Sources. With nearly 100 Illustrations.

Humour, Wit, and Satire of the Seventeenth Century. With nearly 100 Illustrations.

English Caricature and Satire on Napoleon the First. With 115 Illustrations.

Modern Street Ballads. With 57 Illustrations.

** Also a Large Paper Edition of the last (only 100 printed: all numbered), bound in half-parchment. The price of the special copies may be learned from any Bookseller.

Bacteria.—A Synopsis of the Bacteria and Yeast Fungi and Allied Species. By W. B. GROVE, B.A. With 87 Illusts. Crown 8vo, cl. extra, 3s. 6d.

Bankers, A Handbook of London; together with Lists of Bankers from 1677. By F. G. HILTON PRICE. Crown 8vo, cloth extra, 7s. 6d.

Bardsley.—English Surnames: Their Sources and Significations. By Rev. C. W. BARDSLEY, M.A. Third Edition, revised. Crown 8vo, cloth extra, 7s. 6d.

Bartholomew Fair, Memoirs of. By HENRY MORLEY. With 100 Illusts. Crown 8vo, cloth extra, 7s. 6d.

Beaconsfield, Lord: A Biography. By T. P. O'CONNOR, M.P. Sixth Edition, with a New Preface. Crown 8vo, cloth extra, 7s. 6d.

Beerbohm. — Wanderings in Patagonia; or, Life among the Ostrich Hunters. By JULIUS BEERBOHM. With Illusts. Crown 8vo, cloth extra, 3s. 6d.

Belgravia for 1888. One Shilling Monthly. Two New Serial Stories began in BELGRAVIA for JANUARY, and will be continued through the year: Undercurrents, by the Author of "Phyllis;" and The Blackhall Ghosts, by SARAH TYTLER.

** *Bound Volumes from the beginning are kept in stock, cloth extra, gilt edges, 7s. 6d. each; cases for binding Vols., 2s. each.*

Belgravia Holiday Number, published Annually in JULY; and Belgravia Annual, published Annually in NOVEMBER. Each Complete in itself. Demy 8vo, with Illustrations, 1s. each.

Bennett (W.C., LL.D.), Works by: Post 8vo, cloth limp, 2s. each.
A Ballad History of England.
Songs for Sailors.

Besant (Walter) and James Rice, Novels by. Crown 8vo, cloth extra, 3s. 6d. each; post 8vo, illust. boards, 2s. each; cloth limp, 2s. 6d. each.

Ready-Money Mortiboy.
With Harp and Crown.
This Son of Vulcan.
My Little Girl.
The Case of Mr. Lucraft.
The Golden Butterfly.
By Celia's Arbour.
The Monks of Thelema.
'Twas in Trafalgar's Bay.
The Seamy Side.
The Ten Years' Tenant.
The Chaplain of the Fleet.

Besant (Walter), Novels by:
Crown 8vo, cloth extra, 3s. 6d. each;
post 8vo, illust. boards, 2s. each;
cloth limp, 2s. 6d. each.

All Sorts and Conditions of Men:
An Impossible Story. With Illustrations by FRED. BARNARD.

The Captains' Room, &c. With
Frontispiece by E. J. WHEELER.

All in a Garden Fair. With 6 Illustrations by HARRY FURNISS.

Dorothy Forster. With Frontispiece by CHARLES GREEN.

Uncle Jack, and other Stories.

Children of Gibeon.

Crown 8vo, cloth extra, 3s. 6d. each.
The World Went Very Well Then.
With Illustrations by A. FORESTIER.

Herr Paulus: His Rise, his Greatness, and his Fall.

Fifty Years Ago. With One Hundred
and Thirty-seven full-page Plates
and Woodcuts. Demy 8vo, cloth
extra, 16s.

The Eulogy of Richard Jefferies:
A Memoir. With Photograph Portrait. Cr. 8vo, cl. extra, 6s. [*Shortly.*

For Faith and Freedom. Three
Vols., crown 8vo. [*Shortly.*

The Art of Fiction. Demy 8vo, 1s.

Library Edition of the Novels of
Besant and Rice.
*The Volumes are printed from new
type on a large crown 8vo page, and
handsomely bound in cloth. Price Six
Shillings each.*
1. Ready-Money Mortiboy. With Portrait of JAMES RICE, etched by
DANIEL A. WEHRSCHMIDT, and a
New Preface by WALTER BESANT
2. My Little Girl.
3. With Harp and Crown.
4. This Son of Vulcan.
5. The Golden Butterfly. With Etched
Portrait of WALTER BESANT.
6. The Monks of Thelema.
7. By Celia's Arbour.
8. The Chaplain of the Fleet.
9. The Seamy Side.
10. The Case of Mr. Lucraft, &c.
11. 'Twas in Trafalgar's Bay, &c.
12. The Ten Years' Tenant, &c.

Betham-Edwards (M.), Novels
by:
Felicia. Cr. 8vo, cloth extra, 3s. 6d.;
post 8vo, illust. bds., 2s.
Kitty. Post 8vo, illust. bds., 2s.

Bewick (Thomas) and his
Pupils. By AUSTIN DOBSON. With 95
Illusts. Square 8vo, cloth extra, 10s. 6d.

Birthday Books:—
The Starry Heavens: A Poetical
Birthday Book. Square 8vo, handsomely bound in cloth, 2s. 6d.
The Lowell Birthday Book. With
Illusts. Small 8vo, cloth extra, 4s. 6d.

Blackburn's (Henry) Art Handbooks. Demy 8vo, Illustrated, uniform in size for binding.
Academy Notes, separate years, from
1876 to 1887, each 1s.
Academy Notes, 1888. With numerous Illustrations. 1s.
Academy Notes, 1880–84 Complete
in One Volume, with about 700 Facsimile Illustrations. Cloth limp, 6s.
Grosvenor Notes, 1877. 6d.
Grosvenor Notes, separate years, from
1878 to 1887, each 1s.
Grosvenor Notes, 1888. With numerous Illusts. 1s.
Grosvenor Notes, Vol. I., 1877–82.
With upwards of 300 Illustrations.
Demy 8vo, cloth limp, 6s.
Grosvenor Notes, Vol. II., 1883–87.
With upwards of 300 Illustrations.
Demy 8vo, cloth limp, 6s.
The New Gallery, 1888. With numerous Illustrations. 1s.
The English Pictures at the National
Gallery. 114 Illustrations. 1s.
The Old Masters at the National
Gallery. 128 Illustrations. 1s. 6d.
A Complete Illustrated Catalogue
to the National Gallery. With
Notes by H. BLACKBURN, and 242
Illusts. Demy 8vo, cloth limp, 3s.

The Paris Salon, 1888. With 300 Facsimile Sketches. Demy 8vo, 3s.

Blake (William): Etchings from
his Works. By W. B. SCOTT. With
descriptive Text. Folio, half-bound
boards, India Proofs, 21s.

Boccaccio's Decameron; or,
Ten Days' Entertainment. Translated
into English, with an Introduction by
THOMAS WRIGHT, F.S.A. With Portrait
and STOTHARD's beautiful Copperplates. Cr. 8vo, cloth extra, gilt, 7s. 6d.

Bourne (H. R. Fox), Works by:
English Merchants: Memoirs in Illustration of the Progress of British
Commerce. With numerous Illustrations. Cr. 8vo, cloth extra, 7s. 6d.
English Newspapers: Chapters in
the History of Journalism. Two
Vols., demy 8vo, cloth extra, 25s.

Bowers'(G.) Hunting Sketches:
Oblong 4to, half-bound boards, 21s. each
Canters in Crampshire.
Leaves from a Hunting Journal
Coloured in facsimile of the originals

Boyle (Frederick), Works by :
Crown 8vo, cloth extra, 3s. 6d. each; post 8vo, illustrated boards, 2s. each.
Camp Notes: Stories of Sport and Adventure in Asia, Africa, America.
Savage Life : Adventures of a Globe-Trotter.

Chronicles of No-Man's Land. Post 8vo, illust. boards, 2s.

Brand's Observations on Popular Antiquities, chiefly Illustrating the Origin of our Vulgar Customs, Ceremonies, and Superstitions. With the Additions of Sir HENRY ELLIS. Crown 8vo, with Illustrations, 7s. 6d.

Bret Harte, Works by :
Bret Harte's Collected Works. Arranged and Revised by the Author. Complete in Five Vols., crown 8vo, cloth extra, 6s. each.
  Vol. I. COMPLETE POETICAL AND DRAMATIC WORKS. With Steel Portrait, and Introduction by Author.
  Vol. II. EARLIER PAPERS—LUCK OF ROARING CAMP, and other Sketches —BOHEMIAN PAPERS — SPANISH AND AMERICAN LEGENDS.
  Vol. III. TALES OF THE ARGONAUTS —EASTERN SKETCHES.
  Vol. IV. GABRIEL CONROY.
  Vol. V. STORIES — CONDENSED NOVELS, &c.
The Select Works of Bret Harte, in Prose and Poetry. With Introductory Essay by J. M. BELLEW, Portrait of the Author, and 50 Illustrations. Crown 8vo, cloth extra. 7s. 6d.
Bret Harte's Complete Poetical Works. Author's Copyright Edition. Printed on hand-made paper and bound in buckram. Cr. 8vo, 4s. 6d.
Gabriel Conroy : A Novel. Post 8vo, illustrated boards, 2s.
An Heiress of Red Dog, and other Stories. Post 8vo, illust. boards, 2s.
The Twins of Table Mountain. Fcap. 8vo, picture cover, 1s.
Luck of Roaring Camp, and other Sketches. Post 8vo, illust. bds., 2s.
Jeff Briggs's Love Story. Fcap. 8vo, picture cover, 1s.
Flip. Post 8vo, illust. bds., 2s.; cl. 2s. 6d.
Californian Stories (including THE TWINS OF TABLE MOUNTAIN, JEFF BRIGGS'S LOVE STORY, &c.) Post 8vo, illustrated boards, 2s.
Maruja : A Novel. Post 8vo, illust. boards, 2s.; cloth limp, 2s. 6d.
The Queen of the Pirate Isle. With 28 original Drawings by KATE GREENAWAY, Reproduced in Colours by EDMUND EVANS. Sm. 4to, bds., 5s.
A Phyllis of the Sierras, &c. Post 8vo, Illust. bds., 2s.; cloth limp, 2s. 6d.

Brewer (Rev. Dr.), Works by :
The Reader's Handbook of Allusions, References, Plots, and Stories. Twelfth Thousand. With Appendix, containing a COMPLETE ENGLISH BIBLIOGRAPHY. Cr. 8vo, cloth 7s. 6d.
Authors and their Works, with the Dates: Being the Appendices to "The Reader's Handbook," separately printed. Cr. 8vo, cloth, 2s.
A Dictionary of Miracles: Imitative, Realistic, and Dogmatic. Crown 8vo, cloth extra, 7s. 6d.; half-bound, 9s.

Brewster (Sir David), Works by:
More Worlds than One: The Creed of the Philosopher, and the Hope of the Christian. With Plates. Post 8vo, cloth extra, 4s. 6d.
The Martyrs of Science: Lives of GALILEO, TYCHO BRAHE, and KEPLER. With Portraits. Post 8vo, cloth extra, 4s. 6d.
Letters on Natural Magic. A New Edition, with numerous Illustrations, and Chapters on the Being and Faculties of Man, and Additional Phenomena of Natural Magic, by J. A. SMITH. Post 8vo, cl. ex., 4s. 6d.

Brillat-Savarin.—Gastronomy as a Fine Art. By BRILLAT-SAVARIN. Translated by R. E. ANDERSON, M.A. Post 8vo, cloth limp, 2s. 6d.

Brydges. — Uncle Sam at Home. By HAROLD BRYDGES. Post 8vo, illust. boards, 2s.; cloth, 2s. 6d.

Buchanan's (Robert) Works :
Crown 8vo, cloth extra, 6s. each.
Ballads of Life, Love, and Humour. With a Frontispiece by ARTHUR HUGHES.
Selected Poems of Robert Buchanan. With a Frontispiece by T. DALZIEL.
The Earthquake; or, Six Days and a Sabbath.
The City of Dream: An Epic Poem. With Two Illusts. by P. MACNAB. Second Edition.

Robert Buchanan's Complete Poetical Works. With Steel-plate Portrait. Crown 8vo, cloth extra, 7s. 6d.

Crown 8vo, cloth extra, 3s. 6d. each; post 8vo, illust. boards, 2s. each.
The Shadow of the Sword.
A Child of Nature. With a Frontispiece.
God and the Man. With Illustrations by FRED. BARNARD.
The Martyrdom of Madeline. With Frontispiece by A. W. COOPER.

BUCHANAN (ROBERT), *continued—*
Crown 8vo, cloth extra, 3s. 6d. each;
post 8vo, illustrated boards, 2s. each.
Love Me for Ever. With a Frontis-
piece by P. MACNAB.
Annan Water. | **The New Abelard.**
Foxglove Manor.
Matt: A Story of a Caravan.
The Master of the Mine.

The Heir of Linne. Cheaper Edition.
Crown 8vo, cloth extra, 3s. 6d

Burnett (Mrs.), Novels by:
Surly Tim, and other Stories. Post
8vo, illustrated boards, 2s.

Fcap. 8vo, picture cover, 1s. each.
Kathleen Mavourneen.
Lindsay's Luck.
Pretty Polly Pemberton.

Burton (Captain).—The Book
of the Sword: Being a History of the
Sword and its Use in all Countries,
from the Earliest Times. By RICHARD
F. BURTON. With over 400 Illustrations. Square 8vo, cloth extra, 32s.

Burton (Robert):
The Anatomy of Melancholy. A
New Edition, complete, corrected
and enriched by Translations of the
Classical Extracts. Demy 8vo, cloth
extra, 7s. 6d.
Melancholy Anatomised: Being an
Abridgment, for popular use, of BUR-
TON'S ANATOMY OF MELANCHOLY.
Post 8vo, cloth limp, 2s. 6d.

Byron (Lord):
Byron's Letters and Journals. With
Notices of his Life. By THOMAS
MOORE. Cr. 8vo, cloth extra, 7s. 6d.
Prose and Verse, Humorous, Satiri-
cal, and Sentimental, by THOMAS
MOORE; with Suppressed Passages
from the Memoirs of Lord Byron.
Edited, with Notes and Introduction,
by R. HERNE SHEPHERD. Crown
8vo, cloth extra, 7s. 6d.

Caine (T. Hall), Novels by:
Crown 8vo, cloth extra, 3s. 6d. each; post
8vo, illustrated boards, 2s. each.
The Shadow of a Crime.
A Son of Hagar.

The Deemster: A Romance of the
Isle of Man. Fourth Edition, crown
8vo, cloth extra, 3s. 6d.

Cameron (Commander).—
The Cruise of the "Black Prince"
Privateer, Commanded by ROBERT
HAWKINS, Master Mariner. By V.
LOVETT CAMERON, R.N., C.B., D.C.L.
With Frontispiece and Vignette by P.
MACNAB. Crown 8vo, cl. ex., 5s.; post
8vo, illustrated boards, 2s.

Cameron (Mrs. H. Lovett),
Novels by:
Crown 8vo, cloth extra, 3s. 6d. each
post 8vo, illustrated boards, 2s. each.
Juliet's Guardian. | Deceivers Ever.

Carlyle (Thomas):
On the Choice of Books. By THOMAS
CARLYLE. With a Life of the Author
by R. H. SHEPHERD. New and Re-
vised Edition, post 8vo, cloth extra,
Illustrated, 1s. 6d.
The Correspondence of Thomas
Carlyle and Ralph Waldo Emerson,
1834 to 1872. Edited by CHARLES
ELIOT NORTON. With Portraits. Two
Vols., crown 8vo, cloth extra, 24s.

Chapman's (George) Works:
Vol. I. contains the Plays complete,
including the doubtful ones. Vol. II.,
the Poems and Minor Translations,
with an Introductory Essay by ALGER-
NON CHARLES SWINBURNE. Vol. III.,
the Translations of the Iliad and Odyssey. Three Vols., crown 8vo, cloth
extra, 18s.; or separately, 6s. each.

Chatto & Jackson.—A Treatise
on Wood Engraving, Historical and
Practical. By WM. ANDREW CHATTO
and JOHN JACKSON. With an Additional Chapter by HENRY G. BOHN;
and 450 fine Illustrations. A Reprint
of the last Revised Edition. Large
4to, half-bound, 28s.

Chaucer:
Chaucer for Children: A Golden
Key. By Mrs. H.R. HAWEIS. With
Eight Coloured Pictures and nu-
merous Woodcuts by the Author.
New Ed., small 4to, cloth extra, 6s.
Chaucer for Schools. By Mrs. H. R.
HAWEIS. Demy 8vo, cloth limp, 2s.6d.

Chronicle (The) of the Coach:
Charing Cross to Ilfracombe. By J. D
CHAMPLIN. With 75 Illustrations by
EDWARD L. CHICHESTER. Square 8vo,
cloth extra, 7s. 6d.

Clodd.—Myths and Dreams.
By EDWARD CLODD, F.R.A.S., Author
of "The Story of Creation," &c.
Crown 8vo, cloth extra, 5s.

Cobban.—The Cure of Souls:
A Story. By J. MACLAREN COBBAN.
Post 8vo, illustrated boards, 2s.

Coleman (John), Works by:
Curly: An Actor's Story. Illustrated
by J. C. DOLLMAN. Crown 8vo, 1s.;
cloth, 1s. 6d.
Players and Playwrights I have
Known. Two Vols., demy 8vo, cloth
extra, 24s. [*Shortly.*

Collins (Wilkie), Novels by :

Crown 8vo, cloth extra, 3s. 6d. each ; post 8vo, illustrated boards, 2s. each; cloth limp, 2s. 6d. each.

Antonina. Illust. by Sir JOHN GILBERT.

Basil. Illustrated by Sir JOHN GILBERT and J. MAHONEY.

Hide and Seek. Illustrated by Sir JOHN GILBERT and J. MAHONEY.

The Dead Secret. Illustrated by Sir JOHN GILBERT.

Queen of Hearts. Illustrated by Sir JOHN GILBERT.

My Miscellanies. With a Steel-plate Portrait of WILKIE COLLINS.

The Woman in White. With Illustrations by Sir JOHN GILBERT and F. A. FRASER.

The Moonstone. With Illustrations by G. DU MAURIER and F. A. FRASER.

Man and Wife. Illust. by W. SMALL.

Poor Miss Finch. Illustrated by G. DU MAURIER and EDWARD HUGHES.

Miss or Mrs. ? With Illustrations by S. L. FILDES and HENRY WOODS.

The New Magdalen. Illustrated by G. DU MAURIER and C. S. REINHARDT.

The Frozen Deep. Illustrated by G. DU MAURIER and J. MAHONEY.

The Law and the Lady. Illustrated by S. L. FILDES and SYDNEY HALL.

The Two Destinies.

The Haunted Hotel. Illustrated by ARTHUR HOPKINS.

The Fallen Leaves.

Jezebel's Daughter.

The Black Robe.

Heart and Science: A Story of the Present Time.

"I Say No."

The Evil Genius.

Little Novels. Cr. 8vo, cl. ex., 3s. 6d.

The Legacy of Cain. Three Vols., crown 8vo. [*Dec.*

Collins (Mortimer), Novels by :

Crown 8vo, cloth extra, 3s. 6d. each ; post 8vo, illustrated boards, 2s. each.

Sweet Anne Page. | Transmigration.

From Midnight to Midnight.

A Fight with Fortune. Post 8vo, illustrated boards, 2s.

Collins (Mortimer & Frances), Novels by :

Crown 8vo, cloth extra, 3s. 6d. each; post 8vo, illustrated boards, 2s. each.

Blacksmith and Scholar.

The Village Comedy.

You Play Me False.

Post 8vo, illustrated boards, 2s. each.

Sweet and Twenty. | Frances.

Collins (C. Allston).—The Bar Sinister: A Story. By C. ALLSTON COLLINS. Post 8vo, illustrated bds., 2s.

Colman's Humorous Works :

"Broad Grins," "My Nightgown and Slippers," and other Humorous Works, Prose and Poetical, of GEORGE COLMAN. With Life by G. B. BUCKSTONE, and Frontispiece by HOGARTH. Crown 8vo cloth extra, gilt, 7s. 6d.

Colquhoun.—Every Inch a Soldier : A Novel. By M. J. COLQUHOUN. Cheaper Edition. Post 8vo, illustrated boards, 2s. [*Shortly.*

Convalescent Cookery : A Family Handbook. By CATHERINE RYAN. Crown 8vo, 1s. ; cloth, 1s. 6d.

Conway (Moncure D.), Works by :

Demonology and Devil-Lore. Two Vols., royal 8vo, with 65 Illusts., 28s.

A Necklace of Stories. Illustrated by W. J. HENNESSY. Square 8vo, cloth extra, 6s.

Pine and Palm: A Novel. Cheaper Edition. Post 8vo, illustrated boards, 2s. [*Preparing.*

Cook (Dutton), Novels by :

Leo. Post 8vo, illustrated boards, 2s.

Paul Foster's Daughter. Crown 8vo, cloth extra, 3s. 6d. ; post 8vo, illustrated boards, 2s.

Copyright. —A Handbook of English and Foreign Copyright in Literary and Dramatic Works. By SIDNEY JERROLD. Post 8vo, cl., 2s. 6d.

Cornwall.—Popular Romances of the West of England; or, The Drolls, Traditions, and Superstitions of Old Cornwall. Collected and Edited by ROBERT HUNT, F.R.S. New and Revised Edition, with Additions, and Two Steel-plate Illustrations by GEORGE CRUIKSHANK. Crown 8vo, cloth extra, 7s. 6d.

Craddock. — The Prophet of the Great Smoky Mountains. By CHARLES EGBERT CRADDOCK. Post 8vo illust. bds., 2s, cloth limp, 2s. 6d.

Cruikshank (George):
The Comic Almanack. Complete in Two SERIES: The FIRST from 1835 to 1843; the SECOND from 1844 to 1853. A Gathering of the BEST HUMOUR of THACKERAY, HOOD, MAYHEW, ALBERT SMITH, A'BECKETT, ROBERT BROUGH, &c. With 2,000 Woodcuts and Steel Engravings by CRUIKSHANK, HINE, LANDELLS, &c. Crown 8vo, cloth gilt, two very thick volumes, 7s. 6d. each.
The Life of George Cruikshank. By BLANCHARD JERROLD, Author of "The Life of Napoleon III.," &c. With 84 Illustrations. New and Cheaper Edition, enlarged, with Additional Plates, and a very carefully compiled Bibliography. Crown 8vo, cloth extra, 7s. 6d.

Cumming (C. F. Gordon), Works by:
Demy 8vo, cloth extra, 8s. 6d. each.
In the Hebrides. With Autotype Facsimile and numerous full-page Illusts.
In the Himalayas and on the Indian Plains. With numerous Illustrations.
Via Cornwall to Egypt. With a Photogravure Frontispiece. Demy 8vo, cloth extra, 7s. 6d.

Cussans.—Handbook of Heraldry; with Instructions for Tracing Pedigrees and Deciphering Ancient MSS., &c. By JOHN E. CUSSANS. Entirely New and Revised Edition, illustrated with over 400 Woodcuts and Coloured Plates. Crown 8vo, cloth extra, 7s. 6d.

Cyples.—Hearts of Gold: A Novel. By WILLIAM CYPLES. Crown 8vo, cloth extra, 3s. 6d.; post 8vo, illustrated boards, 2s.

Daniel. — Merrie England In the Olden Time. By GEORGE DANIEL. With Illustrations by ROBT. CRUIKSHANK. Crown 8vo, cloth extra, 3s. 6d.

Daudet.—The Evangelist; or, Port Salvation. By ALPHONSE DAUDET. Translated by C. HARRY MELTZER. With Portrait of the Author. Crown 8vo, cloth extra, 3s. 6d.; post 8vo, illust. boards, 2s.

Davenant.—Hints for Parents on the Choice of a Profession or Trade for their Sons. By FRANCIS DAVENANT, M.A. Post 8vo, 1s.; cloth limp, 1s. 6d.

Davies (Dr. N. E.), Works by:
Crown 8vo, 1s. each; cloth limp, 1s. 6d. each.
One Thousand Medical Maxims.
Nursery Hints: A Mother's Guide.

Aids to Long Life. Crown 8vo, 2s.; cloth limp, 2s. 6d.

Davies' (Sir John) Complete Poetical Works, including Psalms I. to L. in Verse, and other hitherto Unpublished MSS., for the first time Collected and Edited, with Memorial-Introduction and Notes, by the Rev. A. B. GROSART, D.D. Two Vols., crown 8vo, cloth boards, 12s.

De Maistre.—A Journey Round My Room. By XAVIER DE MAISTRE. Translated by HENRY ATTWELL. Post 8vo, cloth limp, 2s. 6d.

De Mille.—A Castle In Spain: A Novel. By JAMES DE MILLE. With a Frontispiece. Crown 8vo, cloth extra, 3s. 6d.; post 8vo, illust. bds., 2s.

Derwent (Leith), Novels by:
Crown 8vo, cloth extra, 3s. 6d. each; post 8vo, illustrated boards, 2s. each.
Our Lady of Tears. | Circe's Lovers.

Dickens (Charles), Novels by
Post 8vo, illustrated boards, 2s. each.
Sketches by Boz. | Nicholas Nickleby
Pickwick Papers. | Oliver Twist.

The Speeches of Charles Dickens 1841-1870. With a New Bibliography, revised and enlarged. Edited and Prefaced by RICHARD HERNE SHEPHERD. Cr. 8vo, cloth extra, 6s.—Also a SMALLER EDITION, in the *Mayfair Library.* Post 8vo, cloth limp, 2s. 6d.
About England with Dickens. By ALFRED RIMMER. With 57 Illustrations by C. A. VANDERHOOF, ALFRED RIMMER, and others. Sq. 8vo, cloth extra, 7s. 6d.

Dictionaries:
A Dictionary of Miracles: Imitative, Realistic, and Dogmatic. By the Rev. E. C. BREWER, LL.D. Crown 8vo, cloth extra, 7s. 6d.; hf.-bound, 9s.
The Reader's Handbook of Allusions, References, Plots, and Stories. By the Rev. E. C. BREWER, LL.D. With an Appendix, containing a Complete English Bibliography. Eleventh Thousand. Crown 8vo, 1,400 pages, cloth extra, 7s. 6d.
Authors and their Works, with the Dates. Being the Appendices to "The Reader's Handbook," separately printed. By the Rev. Dr BREWER. Crown 8vo, cloth limp, 2s.

DICTIONARIES, *continued—*
Familiar Short Sayings of Great Men. With Historical and Explanatory Notes. By SAMUEL A. BENT, M.A. Fifth Edition, revised and enlarged. Cr. 8vo, cloth extra, 7s. 6d.

A Dictionary of the Drama: Being a comprehensive Guide to the Plays, Playwrights, Players, and Playhouses of the United Kingdom and America, from the Earliest to the Present Times. By W. DAVENPORT ADAMS. A thick volume, crown 8vo, half-bound, 12s. 6d. [*In preparation.*

The Slang Dictionary: Etymological, Historical, and Anecdotal. Crown 8vo, cloth extra, 6s. 6d.

Women of the Day: A Biographical Dictionary. By FRANCES HAYS. Cr. 8vo, cloth extra, 5s.

Words, Facts, and Phrases: A Dictionary of Curious, Quaint, and Out-of-the-Way Matters. By ELIEZER EDWARDS. New and Cheaper Issue. Cr. 8vo, cl. ex., 7s. 6d. ; hf.-bd., 9s.

Diderot.—The Paradox of Acting. Translated, with Annotations, from Diderot's "Le Paradoxe sur le Comédien," by WALTER HERRIES POLLOCK. With a Preface by HENRY IRVING. Cr. 8vo, in parchment, 4s. 6d.

Dobson (W. T.), Works by:
Post 8vo, cloth limp, 2s. 6d. each.
Literary Frivolities, Fancies, Follies, and Frolics. [cities.
Poetical Ingenuities and Eccentri-

Doran. — Memories of our Great Towns; with Anecdotic Gleanings concerning their Worthies and their Oddities. By Dr. JOHN DORAN, F.S.A. With 38 Illusts. New and Cheaper Edit. Cr. 8vo, cl. extra, 7s. 6d.

Drama, A Dictionary of the. Being a comprehensive Guide to the Plays, Playwrights, Players, and Playhouses of the United Kingdom and America, from the Earliest to the Present Times. By W. DAVENPORT ADAMS. (Uniform with BREWER'S "Reader's Handbook.") Crown 8vo, half-bound, 12s. 6d. [*In preparation.*

Dramatists, The Old. Cr. 8vo, cl. ex., Vignette Portraits, 6s. per Vol.
Ben Jonson's Works. With Notes Critical and Explanatory, and a Biographical Memoir by WM. GIFFORD. Edit. by Col. CUNNINGHAM. 3 Vols.
Chapman's Works. Complete in Three Vols. Vol. I. contains the Plays complete, including doubtful ones; Vol. II., Poems and Minor Translations, with Introductory Essay by A. C. SWINBURNE; Vol. III., Translations of the Iliad and Odyssey.

DRAMATISTS, THE OLD, *continued—*
Crown 8vo, cloth extra, Vignette Portraits, 6s. per Volume.
Marlowe's Works. Including his Translations. Edited, with Notes and Introduction, by Col. CUNNINGHAM. One Vol.
Massinger's Plays. From the Text of WILLIAM GIFFORD. Edited by Col. CUNNINGHAM. One Vol.

Dyer. — The Folk - Lore of Plants. By Rev. T. F. THISELTON DYER, M.A. Crown 8vo, cloth extra, 6s. [*Shortly.*

Early English Poets. Edited, with Introductions and Annotations, by Rev. A. B. GROSART, D.D. Crown 8vo, cloth boards, 6s. per Volume.
Fletcher's (Giles, B.D.) Complete Poems. One Vol.
Davies' (Sir John) Complete Poetical Works. Two Vols.
Herrick's (Robert) Complete Collected Poems. Three Vols.
Sidney's (Sir Philip) Complete Poetical Works. Three Vols.
Herbert (Lord) of Cherbury's Poems. Edit., with Introd., by J. CHURTON COLLINS. Cr. 8vo, parchment, 8s.

Edgcumbe. — Zephyrus: A Holiday in Brazil and on the River Plate. By E. R. PEARCE EDGCUMBE. With 41 Illusts. Cr. 8vo, cl. extra, 5s.

Edwardes (Mrs. A.), Novels by:
A Point of Honour. Post 8vo, illustrated boards, 2s.
Archie Lovell. Crown 8vo, cloth extra, 3s. 6d.; post 8vo, illust. bds., 2s.

Eggleston.—Roxy: A Novel. By EDWARD EGGLESTON. Post 8vo, illust. boards, 2s.

Emanuel.—On Diamonds and Precious Stones: their History, Value, and Properties; with Simple Tests for ascertaining their Reality. By HARRY EMANUEL, F.R.G.S. With numerous Illustrations, tinted and plain. Crown 8vo, cloth extra, gilt, 6s.

Ewald (Alex. Charles, F.S.A.), Works by:
The Life and Times of Prince Charles Stuart, Count of Albany, commonly called the Young Pretender. From the State Papers and other Sources. New and Cheaper Edition, with a Portrait, crown 8vo, cloth extra, 7s. 6d.
Stories from the State Papers. With an Autotype Facsimile. Crown 8vo, cloth extra, 6s.
Studies Re-studied: Historical Sketches from Original Sources. Demy 8vo, cloth extra, 12s.

Englishman's House, The: A Practical Guide to all interested in Selecting or Building a House; with full Estimates of Cost, Quantities, &c. By C. J. RICHARDSON. Fourth Edition. With Coloured Frontispiece and nearly 600 Illustrations. Crown 8vo, cloth extra, 7s. 6d.

Eyes, Our: How to Preserve Them from Infancy to Old Age. By JOHN BROWNING, F.R.A.S., &c. Sixth Edition (Eleventh Thousand). With 58 Illustrations. Crown 8vo, cloth, 1s.

Familiar Short Sayings of Great Men. By SAMUEL ARTHUR BENT, A.M. Fifth Edition, Revised and Enlarged. Crown 8vo, cloth extra, 7s. 6d.

Faraday (Michael), Works by:
Post 8vo, cloth extra, 4s. 6d. each.
The Chemical History of a Candle: Lectures delivered before a Juvenile Audience at the Royal Institution. Edited by WILLIAM CROOKES, F.C.S. With numerous Illustrations.
On the Various Forces of Nature, and their Relations to each other: Lectures delivered before a Juvenile Audience at the Royal Institution. Edited by WILLIAM CROOKES, F.C.S. With numerous Illustrations.

Farrer (James Anson), Works by:
Military Manners and Customs. Crown 8vo, cloth extra, 6s.
War: Three Essays, Reprinted from "Military Manners." Crown 8vo, 1s.; cloth, 1s. 6d.

Fin-Bec.—The Cupboard Papers: Observations on the Art of Living and Dining. By FIN-BEC. Post 8vo, cloth limp, 2s. 6d.

Fireworks, The Complete Art of Making; or, The Pyrotechnist's Treasury. By THOMAS KENTISH. With 267 Illustrations. A New Edition, Revised throughout and greatly Enlarged. Crown 8vo, cloth extra, 5s.

Fitzgerald (Percy), Works by:
The World Behind the Scenes. Crown 8vo, cloth extra, 3s. 6d.
Little Essays: Passages from the Letters of CHARLES LAMB. Post 8vo, cloth limp, 2s. 6d.
A Day's Tour: A Journey through France and Belgium. With Sketches in facsimile of the Original Drawings. Crown 4to picture cover, 1s.
Fatal Zero: A Homburg Diary. Cr. 8vo, cloth extra, 3s. 6d.; post 8vo, illustrated boards, 2s.

FITZGERALD (PERCY), *continued—*
Post 8vo, illustrated boards, 2s. each.
Bella Donna. | Never Forgotten.
The Second Mrs. Tillotson.
Seventy-five Brooke Street
Polly. | The Lady of Brantome.

Fletcher's (Giles, B.D.) Complete Poems: Christ's Victorie in Heaven, Christ's Victorie on Earth, Christ's Triumph over Death, and Minor Poems. With Memorial-Introduction and Notes by the Rev. A. B. GROSART, D.D. Cr. 8vo, cloth bds., 6s.

Fonblanque.—Filthy Lucre: A Novel. By ALBANY DE FONBLANQUE. Post 8vo, illustrated boards, 2s.

Francillon (R. E.), Novels by:
Crown 8vo, cloth extra, 3s. 6d. each; post 8vo, illust. boards, 2s. each.
One by One. | A Real Queen.
Queen Cophetua. |

Olympia. Post 8vo, illust. boards, 2s.
Esther's Glove. Fcap. 8vo, 1s.
King or Knave: A Novel. Cheaper Edition. Crown 8vo, cloth extra, 3s. 6d. *[Shortly.*

Frederic. — Seth's Brother's Wife: A Novel. By HAROLD FREDERIC. Cheaper Edition. Post 8vo, illustrated boards, 2s.

French Literature, History of By HENRY VAN LAUN. Complete in 3 Vols., demy 8vo, cl. bds., 7s. 6d. each.

Frere.—Pandurang Hari; or, Memoirs of a Hindoo. With a Preface by Sir H. BARTLE FRERE, G.C.S.I., &c. Crown 8vo, cloth extra, 3s. 6d.; post 8vo, illustrated boards, 2s.

Friswell.—One of Two: A Novel. By HAIN FRISWELL. Post 8vo, illustrated boards, 2s.

Frost (Thomas), Works by:
Crown 8vo, cloth extra, 3s. 6d. each.
Circus Life and Circus Celebrities.
The Lives of the Conjurers.
The Old Showmen and the Old London Fairs.

Fry's (Herbert) Royal Guide to the London Charities, 1887-8. Showing their Name, Date of Foundation, Objects, Income, Officials, &c. Published Annually. Cr. 8vo, cloth, 1s. 6d.

Gardening Books:
A Year's Work in Garden and Greenhouse: Practical Advice to Amateur Gardeners as to the Management of the Flower, Fruit, and Frame Garden. By GEORGE GLENNY. Post 8vo, 1s.; cloth limp, 1s. 6d.

GARDENING BOOKS, *continued—*
Post 8vo, 1s. each; cl. limp, 1s. 6d. each.
Our Kitchen Garden: The Plants we
Grow, and How we Cook Them.
By TOM JERROLD.
Household Horticulture: A Gossip
about Flowers. By TOM and JANE
JERROLD. Illustrated.
The Garden that Paid the Rent.
By TOM JERROLD.

My Garden Wild, and What I Grew
there. By F. G. HEATH. Crown 8vo,
cloth extra, 5s.; gilt edges, 6s.

Garrett.—The Capel Girls: A
Novel. By EDWARD GARRETT. Cr. 8vo,
cl. ex., 3s. 6d.; post 8vo, illust. bds., 2s.

Gentleman's Magazine (The)
for 1888. 1s. Monthly. In addition
to the Articles upon subjects in Literature, Science, and Art, for which this
Magazine has so high a reputation,
"Science Notes," by W. MATTIEU
WILLIAMS, F.R.A.S., and "Table Talk,"
by SYLVANUS URBAN, appear monthly.
  * *Bound Volumes for recent years are
kept in stock, cloth extra, price* 8s. 6d.
each; Cases for binding, 2s. *each.*

Gentleman's Annual (The).
Published Annually in November. In
illuminated cover. Demy 8vo, 1s. The
Number for 1888 is entitled " By Devious Ways," by T. W. SPEIGHT.

German Popular Stories. Col-
lected by the Brothers GRIMM, and
Translated by EDGAR TAYLOR. Edited,
with an Introduction, by JOHN RUSKIN.
With 22 Illustrations on Steel by
GEORGE CRUIKSHANK. Square 8vo,
cloth extra, 6s. 6d.; gilt edges, 7s. 6d.

Gibbon (Charles), Novels by:
Crown 8vo, cloth extra, 3s. 6d. each
post 8vo, illustrated boards, 2s. each.

Robin Gray.	In Honour Bound.
What will the	Braes of Yarrow.
World Say?	A Heart's Prob-
Queen of the	lem.
Meadow.	The GoldenShaft.
The Flower of the	Of High Degree.
Forest.	Loving a Dream.

Post 8vo, illustrated boards, 2s. each.
For Lack of Gold.
For the King. | In Pastures Green.
In Love and War.
By Mead and Stream.
Fancy Free. | A Hard Knot.
Heart's Delight.

Gilbert (William), Novels by:
Post 8vo, illustrated boards, 2s. each.
Dr. Austin's Guests.
The Wizard of the Mountain.
James Duke, Costermonger.

Gilbert (W. S.), Original Plays
by: In Two Series, each complete in
itself, price 2s. 6d. each.
  The FIRST SERIES contains—The
Wicked World—Pygmalion and Ga-
latea — Charity — The Princess — The
Palace of Truth—Trial by Jury.
  The SECOND SERIES contains—Bro-
ken Hearts—Engaged—Sweethearts—
Gretchen—Dan'l Druce—Tom Cobb—
H.M.S. Pinafore—The Sorcerer—The
Pirates of Penzance.

Eight Original Comic Operas. Writ-
ten by W. S. GILBERT. Containing:
The Sorcerer—H.M.S. "Pinafore"
—The Pirates of Penzance—Iolanthe
— Patience — Princess Ida — The
Mikado—Trial by Jury. Demy 8vo,
cloth limp, 2s. 6d.

Glenny.—A Year's Work in
Garden and Greenhouse: Practical
Advice to Amateur Gardeners as to
the Management of the Flower, Fruit,
and Frame Garden. By GEORGE
GLENNY. Post 8vo, 1s.; cloth, 1s. 6d.

Godwin.—Lives of the Necro-
mancers. By WILLIAM GODWIN.
Post 8vo, limp, 2s.

Golden Library, The:
Square 16mo (Tauchnitz size), cloth
limp, 2s. per Volume.
Bayard Taylor's Diversions of the
Echo Club.
Bennett's (Dr. W. C.) Ballad History
of England.
Bennett's (Dr.) Songs for Sailors.
Godwin's (William) Lives of the
Necromancers.
Holmes's Autocrat of the Break-
fast Table. Introduction by SALA.
Holmes's Professor at the Break-
fast Table.
Hood's Whims and Oddities. Com-
plete. All the original Illustrations.
Jesse's (Edward) Scenes and Oc-
cupations of a Country Life.
Lamb's Essays of Elia. Both Series
Complete in One Vol.
Leigh Hunt's Essays: A Tale for a
Chimney Corner, and other Pieces.
With Portrait, and Introduction by
EDMUND OLLIER.
Mallory's (Sir Thomas) Mort
d'Arthur: The Stories of King
Arthur and of the Knights of the
Round Table. Edited by B. MONT-
GOMERIE RANKING.
Square 16mo, 2s. per Volume.
Pascal's Provincial Letters. A New
Translation, with Historical Intro-
duction and Notes, by T. M'CRIE, D.D.
Pope's Poetical Works. Complete.

Horne.—Orion : An Epic Poem, in Three Books. By RICHARD HENGIST HORNE. With Photographic Portrait from a Medallion by SUMMERS. Tenth Edition, crown 8vo, cloth extra, 7s.

Hunt (Mrs. Alfred), Novels by: Crown 8vo, cloth extra, 3s. 6d. each; post 8vo, illustrated boards, 2s. each.
  Thornicroft's Model.
  The Leaden Casket.
  Self-Condemned.
  That other Person.

Hunt.—Essays by Leigh Hunt. A Tale for a Chimney Corner, and other Pieces. With Portrait and Introduction by EDMUND OLLIER. Post 8vo, cloth limp, 2s.

Hydrophobia: an Account of M. PASTEUR'S System. Containing a Translation of all his Communications on the Subject, the Technique of his Method, and the latest Statistical Results. By RENAUD SUZOR, M.B., C.M. Edin., and M.D. Paris, Commissioned by the Government of the Colony of Mauritius to study M. PASTEUR'S new Treatment in Paris. With 7 Illusts. Cr. 8vo, cloth extra, 6s.

Indoor Paupers. By ONE OF THEM. Crown 8vo, 1s.; cloth, 1s. 6d.

Ingelow.—Fated to be Free: A Novel. By JEAN INGELOW. Crown 8vo, cloth extra, 3s. 6d.; post 8vo, illustrated boards, 2s.

Irish Wit and Humour, Songs of. Collected and Edited by A. PERCEVAL GRAVES. Post 8vo, cloth limp, 2s. 6d.

James.—A Romance of the Queen's Hounds. By CHARLES JAMES. Post 8vo, picture cover, 1s.; cl., 1s. 6d.

Janvier.—Practical Keramics for Students. By CATHERINE A. JANVIER. Crown 8vo, cloth extra, 6s.

Jay (Harriett), Novels by: Post 8vo, illustrated boards, 2s. each.
  The Dark Colleen.
  The Queen of Connaught.

Jefferies (Richard), Works by: Nature near London. Crown 8vo, cl. ex, 6s.; post 8vo, cl. limp, 2s. 6d.
The Life of the Fields. Post 8vo, cloth limp, 2s. 6d.
The Open Air. Crown 8vo, cloth extra, 6s.

The Eulogy of Richard Jefferies. By WALTER BESANT. With a Photograph Portrait and facsimile of Signature. Cr. 8vo, cl. ex., 6s. [*Shortly.*

Jennings (H. J.), Works by: Curiosities of Criticism. Post 8vo, cloth limp, 2s. 6d.
Lord Tennyson: A Biographical Sketch. With a Photograph-Portrait. Crown 8vo, cloth extra, 6s.

Jerrold (Tom), Works by: Post 8vo, 1s. each; cloth, 1s. 6d. each.
The Garden that Paid the Rent.
Household Horticulture: A Gossip about Flowers. Illustrated.
Our Kitchen Garden: The Plants we Grow, and How we Cook Them.

Jesse.—Scenes and Occupations of a Country Life. By EDWARD JESSE. Post 8vo, cloth limp, 2s.

Jeux d'Esprit. Collected and Edited by HENRY S. LEIGH. Post 8vo, cloth limp, 2s. 6d.

"John Herring," Novels by the Author of:
Crown 8vo, cloth extra, 3s. 6d. each.
Red Spider. | Eve.

Jones (Wm., F.S.A.), Works by: Crown 8vo, cloth extra, 7s. 6d. each.
Finger-Ring Lore: Historical, Legendary, and Anecdotal. With over Two Hundred Illustrations.
Credulities, Past and Present; including the Sea and Seamen, Miners, Talismans, Word and Letter Divination, Exorcising and Blessing of Animals, Birds, Eggs, Luck, &c. With an Etched Frontispiece.
Crowns and Coronations: A History of Regalia in all Times and Countries. One Hundred Illustrations.

Jonson's (Ben) Works. With Notes Critical and Explanatory, and a Biographical Memoir by WILLIAM GIFFORD. Edited by Colonel CUNNINGHAM. Three Vols., crown 8vo, cloth extra, 18s.; or separately, 6s. each.

Josephus, The Complete Works of. Translated by WHISTON. Containing both "The Antiquities of the Jews" and "The Wars of the Jews." Two Vols., 8vo, with 52 Illustrations and Maps, cloth extra, gilt, 14s.

Kempt.—Pencil and Palette: Chapters on Art and Artists. By ROBERT KEMPT. Post 8vo, cloth limp, 2s. 6d.

Kershaw.—Colonial Facts and Fictions: Humorous Sketches. By MARK KERSHAW. Post 8vo, illustrated boards, 2s.; cloth, 2s. 6d.

King (R. Ashe), Novels by: Crown 8vo, cloth extra, 3s. 6d. each; post 8vo, illustrated boards, 2s. each.
A Drawn Game.
"The Wearing of the Green."

Kingsley (Henry), Novels by :

Oakshott Castle. Post 8vo, illustrated boards, 2s.

Number Seventeen. Crown 8vo, cloth extra, 3s. 6d.

Knight.—The Patient's Vade

Mecum : How to get most Benefit from Medical Advice. By WILLIAM KNIGHT, M.R.C.S., and EDWARD KNIGHT, L.R.C.P. Crown 8vo, 1s. ; cloth, 1s. 6d.

Lamb (Charles):

Lamb's Complete Works, in Prose and Verse, reprinted from the Original Editions, with many Pieces hitherto unpublished. Edited, with Notes and Introduction, by R. H. SHEPHERD. With Two Portraits and Facsimile of Page of the "Essay on Roast Pig." Cr. 8vo, cl. extra, 7s. 6d.

The Essays of Elia. Complete Edition. Post 8vo, cloth extra, 2s.

Poetry for Children, and Prince Dorus. By CHARLES LAMB. Carefully reprinted from unique copies. Small 8vo, cloth extra, 5s.

Little Essays : Sketches and Characters. By CHARLES LAMB. Selected from his Letters by PERCY FITZGERALD. Post 8vo, cloth limp, 2s. 6d.

Lane's Arabian Nights.—The

Thousand and One Nights: commonly called, in England, "THE ARABIAN NIGHTS' ENTERTAINMENTS." A New Translation from the Arabic with copious Notes, by EDWARD WILLIAM LANE. Illustrated by many hundred Engravings on Wood, from Original Designs by WM. HARVEY. A New Edition, from a Copy annotated by the Translator, edited by his Nephew, EDWARD STANLEY POOLE. With a Preface by STANLEY LANE-POOLE. Three Vols., demy 8vo, cloth extra, 7s. 6d. each.

Lares and Penates ; or, The

Background of Life. By FLORENCE CADDY. Crown 8vo, cloth extra, 6s.

Larwood (Jacob), Works by :

The Story of the London Parks. With Illusts. Cr. 8vo, cl. ex., 3s. 6d.

Post 8vo, cloth limp, 2s. 6d. each.

Forensic Anecdotes.

Theatrical Anecdotes.

Leigh (Henry S.), Works by :

Carols of Cockayne. A New Edition, printed on fcap. 8vo, hand-made paper, and bound in buckram, 5s.

Jeux d'Esprit. Collected and Edited by HENRY S. LEIGH. Post 8vo, cloth limp, 2s. 6d.

Leys.—The Lindsays : A Ro-

mance of Scottish Life. By JOHN K. LEYS. Cheaper Edition. Post 8vo, illustrated boards, 2s.   [Shortly.

Life in London ; or, The History

of Jerry Hawthorn and Corinthian Tom. With the whole of CRUIKSHANK's Illustrations, in Colours, after the Originals. Cr. 8vo, cl. extra, 7s. 6d.

Linskill.—In Exchange for a

Soul. By MARY LINSKILL, Author of "The Haven Under the Hill," &c. Cheaper Edit. Post 8vo, illust. bds., 2s.

Linton (E. Lynn), Works by :

Post 8vo, cloth limp, 2s. 6d. each.

Witch Stories.

The True Story of Joshua Davidson

Ourselves : Essays on Women.

Crown 8vo, cloth extra, 3s. 6d. each ; post 8vo, illustrated boards, 2s. each.

Patricia Kemball.

The Atonement of Leam Dundas.

The World Well Lost.

Under which Lord ?

"My Love ! " | Ione.

Post 8vo, illustrated boards, 2s. each.

With a Silken Thread.

The Rebel of the Family.

Paston Carew, Millionaire and Miser. Crown 8vo, cl. extra, 3s. 6d.

Longfellow's Poetical Works.

Carefully Reprinted from the Original Editions. With numerous fine Illustrations on Steel and Wood. Crown 8vo, cloth extra, 7s. 6d.

Long Life, Aids to: A Medical,

Dietetic, and General Guide in Health and Disease. By N. E. DAVIES, L.R.C.P. Cr. 8vo, 2s. ; cl. limp, 2s. 6d.

Lucy.—Gideon Fleyce: A Novel.

By HENRY W. LUCY. Crown 8vo, cl. ex., 3s. 6d.; post 8vo, illust. bds., 2s.

Lusiad (The) of Camoens.

Translated into English Spenserian Verse by ROBERT FFRENCH DUFF Demy 8vo, with Fourteen full-page Plates, cloth boards, 18s

Macalpine (Avery), Novels by :

Teresa Itasca, and other Stories. Crown 8vo, bound in canvas, 2s. 6d.

Broken Wings. With Illustrations by W. J. HENNESSY. Crown 8vo, cloth extra, 6s.

McCarthy (Justin, M.P.), Works by:

A History of Our Own Times from the Accession of Queen Victoria to the General Election of 1880. Four Vols. demy 8vo, cloth extra, 12s. each.—Also a POPULAR EDITION, in Four Vols. cr. 8vo, cl. extra, 6s. each. —And a JUBILEE EDITION, with an Appendix of Events to the end of 1886, complete in Two Vols., square 8vo, cloth extra, 7s. 6d. each.

A Short History of Our Own Times. One Vol., crown 8vo, cloth extra, 6s.

History of the Four Georges. Four Vols. demy 8vo, cloth extra, 12s. each. [Vol. I. *now ready.*

Crown 8vo, cloth extra, 3s. 6d. each; post 8vo, illustrated boards, 2s. each.

Dear Lady Disdain.
The Waterdale Neighbours.
A Fair Saxon.
Miss Misanthrope.
Donna Quixote.
The Comet of a Season.
Maid of Athens.
Camlola: A Girl with a Fortune.

Post 8vo, illustrated boards, 2s. each.
Linley Rochford.
My Enemy's Daughter.

"The Right Honourable:" A Romance of Society and Politics. By JUSTIN MCCARTHY, M.P., and Mrs. CAMPBELL-PRAED. New and Cheaper Edition, crown 8vo, cloth extra, 6s.

McCarthy (Justin H., M.P.), Works by:

An Outline of the History of Ireland, from the Earliest Times to the Present Day. Cr. 8vo, 1s.; cloth, 1s. 6d.

Ireland since the Union: Sketches of Irish History from 1798 to 1886. Crown 8vo, cloth extra, 6s.

England under Gladstone, 1880-85. Second Edition, revised. Crown 8vo, cloth extra, 6s.

Doom! An Atlantic Episode. Crown 8vo, 1s.; cloth, 1s. 6d.

Our Sensation Novel. Edited by JUSTIN H. MCCARTHY. Crown 8vo, 1s.; cloth, 1s. 6d.

Hafiz in London. Choicely printed. Small 8vo, gold cloth, 3s. 6d.

Magician's Own Book (The):

Performances with Cups and Balls, Eggs Hats, Handkerchiefs, &c. All from actual Experience. Edited by W. H. CREMER. With 200 Illustrations. Crown 8vo, cloth extra, 4s. 6d.

MacDonald.—Works of Fancy and Imagination.

By GEORGE MACDONALD, LL.D. Ten Volumes, in handsome cloth case, 21s. — Vol. 1. WITHIN AND WITHOUT. THE HIDDEN LIFE.— Vol. 2. THE DISCIPLE. THE GOSPEL WOMEN. A BOOK OF SONNETS, ORGAN SONGS.—Vol. 3. VIOLIN SONGS. SONGS OF THE DAYS AND NIGHTS. A BOOK OF DREAMS. ROADSIDE POEMS. POEMS FOR CHILDREN. Vol. 4. PARABLES. BALLADS. SCOTCH SONGS.— Vols. 5 and 6. PHANTASTES: A Faerie Romance.—Vol. 7. THE PORTENT.— Vol. 8. THE LIGHT PRINCESS. THE GIANT'S HEART. SHADOWS.— Vol. 9. CROSS PURPOSES. THE GOLDEN KEY. THE CARASOYN. LITTLE DAYLIGHT.— Vol. 10. THE CRUEL PAINTER. THE WOW O' RIVVEN. THE CASTLE. THE BROKEN SWORDS. THE GRAY WOLF UNCLE CORNELIUS.

The Volumes are also sold separately in Grolier-pattern cloth, 2s. 6d. each.

Macdonell.—Quaker Cousins:

A Novel. By AGNES MACDONELL. Crown 8vo, cloth extra, 3s. 6d.; post 8vo, illustrated boards, 2s.

Macgregor. — Pastimes and Players.

Notes on Popular Games. By ROBERT MACGREGOR. Post 8vo, cloth limp, 2s. 6d.

Mackay.—Interludes and Undertones;

or, Music at Twilight. By CHARLES MACKAY, LL.D. Crown 8vo, cloth extra, 6s.

Maclise Portrait-Gallery (The)

of Illustrious Literary Characters; with Memoirs—Biographical, Critical, Bibliographical, and Anecdotal—illustrative of the Literature of the former half of the Present Century. By WILLIAM BATES, B.A. With 85 Portraits printed on an India Tint. Crown 8vo, cloth extra, 7s. 6d.

Macquoid (Mrs.), Works by:

Square 8vo, cloth extra, 7s. 6d. each.
In the Ardennes. With 50 fine Illustrations by THOMAS R. MACQUOID.
Pictures and Legends from Normandy and Brittany. With numerous Illusts. by THOMAS R. MACQUOID.
Through Normandy. With 90 Illustrations by T. R. MACQUOID.
Through Brittany. With numerous Illustrations by T. R. MACQUOID.
About Yorkshire. With 67 Illustrations by T. R. MACQUOID.

Post 8vo, illustrated boards, 2s. each.
The Evil Eye, and other Stories.
Lost Rose.

Magic Lantern (The), and its
Management: including full Practical Directions for producing the Limelight, making Oxygen Gas, and preparing Lantern Slides. By T. C. HEPWORTH. With 10 Illustrations. Crown 8vo, 1s. ; cloth, 1s. 6d.

Magna Charta.
An exact Facsimile of the Original in the British Museum, printed on fine plate paper, 3 feet by 2 feet, with Arms and Seals emblazoned in Gold and Colours. 5s.

Mallock (W. H.), Works by:
The New Republic; or, Culture, Faith and Philosophy in an English Country House. Post 8vo, cloth limp, 2s. 6d.; Cheap Edition, illustrated boards, 2s.

The New Paul and Virginia; or, Positivism on an Island. Post 8vo, cloth limp, 2s. 6d.

Poems. Small 4to, in parchment, 8s.

Is Life worth Living? Crown 8vo, cloth extra, 6s.

Mallory's (Sir Thomas) Mort
d'Arthur: The Stories of King Arthur and of the Knights of the Round Table. Edited by B. MONTGOMERIE RANKING. Post 8vo, cloth limp, 2s.

Man - Hunter (The):
Stories from the Note-book of a Detective. By DICK DONOVAN. Post 8vo, illustrated boards, 2s.; cloth, 2s. 6d.

Mark Twain, Works by:
The Choice Works of Mark Twain. Revised and Corrected throughout by the Author. With Life, Portrait, and numerous Illust. Cr. 8vo, cl. ex, 7s. 6d.

The Innocents Abroad; or, The New Pilgrim's Progress: Being some Account of the Steamship "Quaker City's" Pleasure Excursion to Europe and the Holy Land. With 234 Illustrations. Crown 8vo, cloth extra, 7s. 6d.—Cheap Edition (under the title of "MARK TWAIN'S PLEASURE TRIP"), post 8vo, illust. boards, 2s.

Roughing It, and The Innocents at Home. With 200 Illustrations by F. A. FRASER. Cr. 8vo, cl. ex., 7s. 6d.

The Gilded Age. By MARK TWAIN and CHARLES DUDLEY WARNER. With 212 Illustrations by T. COPPIN Crown 8vo, cloth extra, 7s. 6d.

The Adventures of Tom Sawyer. With 111 Illustrations. Crown 8vo, cloth extra, 7s. 6d.—Cheap Edition post 8vo, illustrated boards, 2s.

The Prince and the Pauper. With nearly 200 Illustrations. Crown 8vo, cloth extra, 7s. 6d.—Cheap Edition, post 8vo, illustrated boards, 2s.

A Tramp Abroad. With 314 Illusts. Cr. 8vo, cloth extra, 7s. 6d.—Cheap Edition, post 8vo illust. bds., 2s.

MARK TWAIN'S WORKS, continued—
The Stolen White Elephant, &c. Crown 8vo, cloth extra, 6s.; post 8vo, illustrated boards, 2s.

Life on the Mississippi. With about 300 Original Illustrations. Crown 8vo, cloth extra, 7s. 6d.—Cheap Edition, post 8vo, illustrated boards, 2s.

The Adventures of Huckleberry Finn. With 174 Illustrations by E. W. KEMBLE. Crown 8vo, cloth extra, 7s. 6d.—Cheap Edition, post 8vo, illustrated boards, 2s.

Mark Twain's Library of Humour. With numerous Illustrations. Crown 8vo, cloth extra, 7s. 6d.

Marlowe's Works.
Including his Translations. Edited, with Notes and Introductions, by Col. CUNNINGHAM. Crown 8vo, cloth extra, 6s.

Marryat (Florence), Novels by:
Crown 8vo, cloth extra. 3s. 6d. each; post 8vo, illustrated boards, 2s. each.

Open! Sesame! | Written in Fire.

Post 8vo, illustrated boards, 2s. each.

A Harvest of Wild Oats.

Fighting the Air.

Massinger's Plays.
From the Text of WILLIAM GIFFORD. Edited by Col. CUNNINGHAM. Crown 8vo, cloth extra, 6s.

Masterman.—Half a Dozen
Daughters: A Novel. By J. MASTERMAN. Post 8vo, illustrated boards, 2s.

Matthews.—A Secret of the
Sea, &c. By BRANDER MATTHEWS. Post 8vo, illust. bds., 2s. ; cloth, 2s. 6d.

Mayfair Library, The:
Post 8vo, cloth limp, 2s. 6d. per Volume.

A Journey Round My Room. By XAVIER DE MAISTRE. Translated by HENRY ATTWELL.

Quips and Quiddities. Selected by W. DAVENPORT ADAMS.

The Agony Column of "The Times," from 1800 to 1870. Edited, with an Introduction, by ALICE CLAY.

Melancholy Anatomised: A Popular Abridgment of "Burton's Anatomy of Melancholy."

Gastronomy as a Fine Art. By BRILLAT-SAVARIN.

The Speeches of Charles Dickens.

Literary Frivolities, Fancies, Follies, and Frolics. By W. T. DOBSON.

Poetical Ingenuities and Eccentricities. Selected and Edited by W. T. DOBSON.

The Cupboard Papers. By FIN-BEC.

Original Plays by W. S. GILBERT. FIRST SERIES. Containing: The Wicked World — Pygmalion and Galatea—Charity — The Princess—The Palace of Truth—Trial by Jury.

MAYFAIR LIBRARY, *continued—*
Post 8vo, cloth limp, 2s. 6d. per Vol.

Original Plays by W. S GILBERT.
SECOND SERIES. Containing: Broken Hearts — Engaged — Sweethearts—Gretchen—Dan'l Druce—Tom Cobb—H.M.S. Pinafore — The Sorcerer—The Pirates of Penzance.

Songs of Irish Wit and Humour.
Collected and Edited by A. PERCEVAL GRAVES.

Animals and their Masters. By Sir ARTHUR HELPS.

Social Pressure. By Sir A. HELPS.

Curiosities of Criticism. By HENRY J. JENNINGS.

The Autocrat of the Breakfast-Table
By OLIVER WENDELL HOLMES. Illustrated by J. GORDON THOMSON.

Pencil and Palette. By ROBERT KEMPT.

Little Essays: Sketches and Characters. By CHAS. LAMB. Selected from his Letters by PERCY FITZGERALD.

Forensic Anecdotes; or, Humour and Curiosities of the Law and Men of Law. By JACOB LARWOOD.

Theatrical Anecdotes. By JACOB LARWOOD.

Jeux d'Esprit. Edited by HENRY S. LEIGH.

True History of Joshua Davidson. By E. LYNN LINTON.

Witch Stories. By E. LYNN LINTON.

Ourselves: Essays on Women. By E. LYNN LINTON.

Pastimes and Players. By ROBERT MACGREGOR.

The New Paul and Virginia. By W. H. MALLOCK.

New Republic. By W. H. MALLOCK.

Puck on Pegasus. By H. CHOLMONDELEY-PENNELL.

Pegasus Re-Saddled. By H. CHOLMONDELEY-PENNELL. Illustrated by GEORGE DU MAURIER.

Muses of Mayfair. Edited by H. CHOLMONDELEY-PENNELL.

Thoreau: His Life and Aims. By H. A. PAGE.

Puniana. By the Hon. HUGH ROWLEY.

More Puniana. By the Hon. HUGH ROWLEY.

The Philosophy of Handwriting. By DON FELIX DE SALAMANCA.

By Stream and Sea. By WILLIAM SENIOR.

Old Stories Re-told. By WALTER THORNBURY.

Leaves from a Naturalist's Note-Book. By Dr. ANDREW WILSON.

Mayhew.—London Characters
and the Humorous Side of London Life. By HENRY MAYHEW. With numerous Illusts. Cr. 8vo, cl. extra, 3s. 6d.

Medicine, Family.—One Thousand Medical Maxims and Surgical Hints, for Infancy, Adult Life, Middle Age, and Old Age. By N. E. DAVIES, L.R.C.P Lond. Cr. 8vo, 1s.; cl., 1s. 6d.

Menken.—Infelicia: Poems by
ADAH ISAACS MENKEN. A New Edition, with a Biographical Preface, numerous Illustrations by F. E. LUMMIS and F. O. C. DARLEY, and Facsimile of a Letter from CHARLES DICKENS. Beautifully printed on small 4to ivory paper, with red border to each page, and handsomely bound. Price 7s. 6d.

Mexican Mustang (On a),
through Texas, from the Gulf to the Rio Grande. A New Book of American Humour. By A. E. SWEET and J. ARMOY. KNOX, Editors of "Texas Sittings." With 265 Illusts. Cr. 8vo, cl. extra, 7s. 6d.

Middlemass (Jean), Novels by:
Post 8vo, illustrated boards, 2s. each.
Touch and Go. | Mr. Dorillion.

Miller. — Physiology for the
Young; or, The House of Life: Human Physiology, with its application to the Preservation of Health. For Classes and Popular Reading. With numerous Illusts. By Mrs. F. FENWICK MILLER. Small 8vo, cloth limp, 2s. 6d.

Milton (J. L.), Works by:
Sm. 8vo, 1s. each; cloth ex., 1s. 6d. each.
The Hygiene of the Skin. A Concise Set of Rules for the Management of the Skin; with Directions for Diet, Wines, Soaps, Baths, &c.
The Bath in Diseases of the Skin.
The Laws of Life, and their Relation to Diseases of the Skin.

Molesworth (Mrs.).—Hathercourt Rectory. By Mrs. MOLESWORTH, Author of "The Cuckoo Clock," &c. Cr. 8vo, cl. extra, 4s. 6d.; post 8vo, illustrated boards, 2s.

Moncrieff. — The Abdication;
or, Time Tries All. An Historical Drama. By W. D. SCOTT-MONCRIEFF. With Seven Etchings by JOHN PETTIE, R.A., W. Q. ORCHARDSON, R.A., J. MACWHIRTER, A.R.A., COLIN HUNTER, A.R.A., R. MACBETH, A.R.A., and TOM GRAHAM, R.S.A. Large 4to, bound in buckram, 21s.

Moore (Thomas):
Byron's Letters and Journals; with Notices of his Life. By THOMAS MOORE. Cr. 8vo, cloth extra, 7s. 6d.
Prose and Verse, Humorous, Satirical, and Sentimental, by THOMAS MOORE; with Suppressed Passages from the Memoirs of Lord Byron. Edited, with Notes and Introduction, by R. HERNE SHEPHERD. With a Portrait. Cr. 8vo, cloth extra, 7s. 6d.

Murray (D. Christie), Novels
by. Crown 8vo, cloth extra, 3s. 6d. each; post 8vo, illustrated boards, 2s. each.

A Life's Atonement. | A Model Father.
Joseph's Coat. | Coals of Fire.
By the Gate of the Sea.
Val Strange. | Hearts.
The Way of the World.
A Bit of Human Nature.
First Person Singular.
Cynic Fortune.

Old Blazer's Hero. With Three Illustrations by A. McCormick. Crown 8vo, cloth ex., 6s.—Cheaper Edition, post 8vo, illust. boards, 2s. [*Shortly.*
One Traveller Returns. By D. Christie Murray and H. Herman. Cr. 8vo, cl. ex., 6s.

Novelists. — Half-Hours with
the Best Novelists of the Century: Choice Readings from the finest Novels. Edited, with Critical and Biographical Notes, by H. T. Mackenzie Bell. Crown 8vo, cl. ex., 3s. 6d. [*Preparing.*

Nursery Hints: A Mother's
Guide in Health and Disease. By N. E. Davies, L.R.C.P. Cr.8vo, 1s.; cl., 1s.6d.

O'Connor.—Lord Beaconsfield:
A Biography. By T. P. O'Connor, M.P. Sixth Edition, with a New Preface, bringing the work down to the Death of Lord Beaconsfield. Crown 8vo, cloth extra, 7s. 6d.

O'Hanlon. — The Unforeseen:
A Novel. By Alice O'Hanlon. New & Cheaper Ed. Post 8vo, illust. bds., 2s.

Oliphant (Mrs.) Novels by :
Whiteladies. With Illustrations by Arthur Hopkins and H. Woods. Crown 8vo, cloth extra, 3s. 6d.; post 8vo, illustrated boards, 2s.

Crown 8vo, cloth extra, 4s. 6d. each.; post 8vo, illustrated boards, 2s. each.
The Primrose Path.
The Greatest Heiress in England.

O'Reilly.—Phœbe's Fortunes :
A Novel. With Illustrations by Henry Tuck. Post 8vo, illustrated boards, 2s.

O'Shaughnessy (A.), Works by :
Songs of a Worker. Fcap. 8vo, cloth extra, 7s. 6d.
Music and Moonlight. Fcap. 8vo, cloth extra, 7s. 6d.
Lays of France. Cr.8vo, cl. ex.,10s. 6d.

Ouida, Novels by. Crown 8vo,
cloth extra, 3s. 6d. each; post 8vo, illustrated boards, 2s. each.
Held in Bondage. | Under Two Flags.
Strathmore. | Cecil Castle-
Chandos | maine's Gage.

Ouida, *continued—*
Crown 8vo, cloth extra, 3s. 6d. each; post 8vo, illustrated boards, 2s. each.

Idalia. | Friendship.
Tricotrin. | Moths. | Bimbi.
Puck. | Pipistrello.
Folle Farine. | In Maremma.
Two Little Wooden | A Village Com-
Shoes. | mune.
A Dog of Flanders. | Wanda.
Pascarel. | Frescoes. [ine.
Signa. | Ariadne. | Princess Naprax-
In a Winter City. | Othmar.

Wisdom, Wit, and Pathos, selected from the Works of Ouida by F. Sydney Morris. Sm.cr.8vo,cl.ex.,5s.

Page (H. A.), Works by :
Thoreau: His Life and Aims: A Study. With Portrait. Post 8vo,cl.limp, 2s.6d.
Lights on the Way: Some Tales within a Tale. By the late J. H. Alexander, B.A. Edited by H. A. Page. Crown 8vo, cloth extra, 6s.
Animal Anecdotes. Arranged on a New Principle. Cr. 8vo, cl. extra, 5s.

Parliamentary Elections and
Electioneering in the Old Days (A History of). Showing the State of Political Parties and Party Warfare at the Hustings and in the House of Commons from the Stuarts to Queen Victoria. Illustrated from the original Political Squibs, Lampoons, Pictorial Satires, and Popular Caricatures of the Time. By Joseph Grego, Author of "Rowlandson and his Works," "The Life of Gillray," &c. A New Edition, crown 8vo, cloth extra, with Coloured Frontispiece and 100 Illustrations, 7s. 6d. [*Preparing.*

Pascal's Provincial Letters. A
New Translation, with Historical Introduction and Notes, by T. M'Crie, D.D. Post 8vo, cloth limp, 2s.

Patient's (The) Vade Mecum :
How to get most Benefit from Medical Advice. By W. Knight, M.R.C.S., and E. Knight, L.R.C.P. Cr.8vo, 1s.; cl. 1/6.

Paul Ferroll :
Post 8vo, illustrated boards, 2s. each.
Paul Ferroll : A Novel.
Why Paul Ferroll Killed his Wife.

Payn (James), Novels by.
Crown 8vo, cloth extra, 3s. each; post 8vo, illustrated boards, 2s. each.
Lost Sir Massingberd.
Walter's Word.
Less Black than we're Painted.
By Proxy. | High Spirits.
Under One Roof.
A Confidential Agent.

PAYN (JAMES), *continued*—
Some Private Views.
A Grape from a Thorn.
From Exile. | The Canon's Ward.
The Talk of the Town.

Post 8vo, illustrated boards, 2s. each.
Kit: A Memory. | Carlyon's Year.
A Perfect Treasure.
Bentinck's Tutor.|Murphy's Master.
The Best of Husbands.
For Cash Only.
What He Cost Her. | Cecil's Tryst.
Fallen Fortunes. | Halves.
A County Family. | At Her Mercy.
A Woman's Vengeance.
The Clyffards of Clyffe.
The Family Scapegrace.
The Foster Brothers.| Found Dead.
Gwendoline's Harvest.
Humorous Stories.
Like Father, Like Son.
A Marine Residence.
Married Beneath Him.
Mirk Abbey. | Not Wooed, but Won.
Two Hundred Pounds Reward.

Crown 8vo, cloth extra, 3s. 6d. each.
Glow-Worm Tales.
The Mystery of Mirbridge. [*Shortly.*
In Peril and Privation: Stories of
Marine Adventure Re-told. A Book
for Boys. With numerous Illustra-
tions. Crown 8vo, cloth gilt, 6s.
Holiday Tasks. Cr. 8vo, cloth extra,
6s.; post 8vo, illustrated boards, 2s.

Paul.—Gentle and Simple. By
MARGARET AGNES PAUL. With a
Frontispiece by HELEN PATERSON.
Cr. 8vo, cloth extra, 3s. 6d.; post 8vo,
illustrated boards, 2s.

Pears.—The Present Depres-
sion in Trade: Its Causes and Reme-
dies. Being the "Pears" Prize Essays
(of One Hundred Guineas). By EDWIN
GOADBY and WILLIAM WATT. With
an Introductory Paper by Prof. LEONE
LEVI, F.S.A., F.S.S. Demy 8vo, 1s.

Pennell (H. Cholmondeley),
Works by:
Post 8vo, cloth limp, 2s. 6d. each.
Puck on Pegasus. With Illustrations.
Pegasus Re-Saddled. With Ten full-
page Illus. by G. DU MAURIER.
The Muses of Mayfair. Vers de
Société, Selected and Edited by H.
C. PENNELL.

Phelps (E. Stuart), Works by:
Post 8vo, 1s. each; cl. limp, 1s. 6d. each.
Beyond the Gates. By the Author
of "The Gates Ajar."
An Old Maid's Paradise.
Burglars in Paradise.
Jack the Fisherman. With Twenty-
two Illustrations by C. W. REED.
Cr. 8vo, picture cover, 1s.; cl. 1s. 6d.

Pirkis (C. L.), Novels by:
Trooping with Crows. Fcap. 8vo,
picture cover, 1s. [boards, 2s.
Lady Lovelace. Post 8vo, illustrated

Planché (J. R.), Works by:
The Pursuivant of Arms; or, Her-
aldry Founded upon Facts. With
Coloured Frontispiece and 200 Illus-
trations. Cr. 8vo, cloth extra, 7s. 6d.
Songs and Poems, from 1819 to 1879.
Edited, with an Introduction, by his
Daughter, Mrs. MACKARNESS. Crown
8vo, cloth extra, 6s.

Plutarch's Lives of Illustrious
Men. Translated from the Greek,
with Notes Critical and Historical, and
a Life of Plutarch, by JOHN and
WILLIAM LANGHORNE. Two Vols.,
8vo, cloth extra, with Portraits, 10s. 6d.

Poe (Edgar Allan):—
The Choice Works, in Prose and
Poetry, of EDGAR ALLAN POE. With
an Introductory Essay by CHARLES
BAUDELAIRE, Portrait and Fac-
similes. Crown 8vo, cl. extra, 7s. 6d.
The Mystery of Marie Roget, and
other Stories. Post 8vo, illust.bds.,2s.

Pope's Poetical Works. Complete in One Vol. Post 8vo, cl. limp, 2s.

Praed (Mrs. Campbell-).—"The
Right Honourable:" A Romance of
Society and Politics. By Mrs. CAMP-
BELL-PRAED and JUSTIN McCARTHY,
M.P. Cr. 8vo, cloth extra, 6s.

Price (E. C.), Novels by:
Crown 8vo, cloth extra, 3s. 6d. each
post 8vo, illustrated boards, 2s. each.
Valentina. | The Foreigners
Mrs. Lancaster's Rival.
Gerald. Post 8vo, illust. boards, 2s.

Princess Olga—Radna; or, The
Great Conspiracy of 1881. By the
Princess OLGA. Cr. 8vo, cl. ex., 6s.

Proctor (Rich. A.), Works by:
Flowers of the Sky. With 55 Illusts.
Small crown 8vo, cloth extra, 4s. 6d.
Easy Star Lessons. With Star Maps
for Every Night in the Year, Draw-
ings of the Constellations, &c.
Crown 8vo, cloth extra, 6s.
Familiar Science Studies. Crown
8vo, cloth extra, 7s. 6d.
Saturn and Its System. New and
Revised Edition, with 13 Steel Plates.
Demy 8vo, cloth extra, 10s. 6d.
Mysteries of Time and Space. With
Illusts. Cr. 8vo, cloth extra, 7s. 6d.
The Universe of Suns, and other
Science Gleanings. With numerous
Illusts. Cr. 8vo, cloth extra, 7s. 6d.
Wages and Wants of Science
Workers. Crown 8vo, 1s. 6d.

Rabelais' Works. Faithfully
Translated from the French, with
variorum Notes, and numerous characteristic Illustrations by GUSTAVE
DORÉ. Crown 8vo, cloth extra, 7s. 6d.

Rambosson.—Popular Astro-
nomy. By J. RAMBOSSON, Laureate of
the Institute of France. Translated by
C. B. PITMAN. Crown 8vo, cloth gilt,
numerous Illusts., and a beautifully
executed Chart of Spectra, 7s. 6d.

Reade (Charles), Novels by :
Cr. 8vo, cloth extra, illustrated,3s. 6d.
each; post 8vo, illust. bds., 2s. each.
Peg Woffington. Illustrated by S. L.
FILDES, A.R.A.
Christie Johnstone. Illustrated by
WILLIAM SMALL.
It is Never Too Late to Mend. Il-
lustrated by G. I. PINWELL.
**The Course of True Love Never did
run Smooth.** Illustrated by HELEN
PATERSON.
**The Autobiography of a Thief; Jack
of all Trades; and James Lambert.**
Illustrated by MATT STRETCH.
Love me Little, Love me Long. Il-
lustrated by M. ELLEN EDWARDS.
The Double Marriage. Illust. by Sir
JOHN GILBERT, R.A., and C. KEENE.
The Cloister and the Hearth. Il-
lustrated by CHARLES KEENE.
Hard Cash. Illust. by F. W. LAWSON.
Griffith Gaunt. Illustrated by S. L.
FILDES, A.R.A., and WM. SMALL.
Foul Play. Illust. by DU MAURIER.
Put Yourself in His Place. Illus-
trated by ROBERT BARNES.
A Terrible Temptation Illustrated
by EDW. HUGHES and A. W. COOPER.
The Wandering Heir. Illustrated by
H. PATERSON, S. L. FILDES, A.R.A.,
C. GREEN, and H. WOODS, A.R.A.
A Simpleton. Illustrated by KATE
CRAUFORD. [COULDERY.
A Woman-Hater. Illust. by THOS.
Singleheart and Doubleface: A
Matter-of-fact Romance. Illustrated
by P. MACNAB.
**Good Stories of Men and other
Animals.** Illustrated by E. A. ABBEY,
PERCY MACQUOID,and JOSEPH NASH.
The Jilt, and other Stories. Illustrated
by JOSEPH NASH.
Readiana. With a Steel-plate Portrait
of CHARLES READE.

Bible Characters: Studies of David,
Nehemiah, Jonah, &c. Fcap. 8vo,
leatherette, 1s.

Reader's Handbook (The) of
Allusions, References, Plots, and
Stories. By the Rev. Dr. BREWER.
Fifth Edition, revised throughout,
with a New Appendix, containing a
COMPLETE ENGLISH BIBLIOGRAPHY.
Cr. 8vo, 1,400 pages, cloth extra, 7s. 6d.

Rice (Portrait of James).—
Specially etched by DANIEL A. WEHR-
SCHMIDT for the New Library Edition
of BESANT and RICE's Novels. A few
Proofs before Letters have been taken
on Japanese paper, size 15¾ x 10 in.
Price 5s. each.

Richardson. — A Ministry of
Health, and other Papers. By BEN-
JAMIN WARD RICHARDSON, M.D., &c.
Crown 8vo, cloth extra, 6s.

Riddell (Mrs. J. H.), Novels by :
Crown 8vo, cloth extra, 3s. 6d. each ;
post 8vo, illustrated boards, 2s. each.
Her Mother's Darling.
The Prince of Wales's Garden Party.
Weird Stories.

Post 8vo, illustrated boards, 2s. each.
The Uninhabited House.
Fairy Water.
The Mystery in Palace Gardens.

Rimmer (Alfred), Works by :
Square 8vo, cloth gilt, 7s. 6d. each.
Our Old Country Towns. With over
50 Illustrations.
Rambles Round Eton and Harrow.
With 50 Illustrations.
About England with Dickens. With
58 Illustrations by ALFRED RIMMER
and C. A. VANDERHOOF.

Robinson (F. W.), Novels by :
Crown 8vo, cloth extra, 3s. 6d. each ;
post 8vo, illustrated boards, 2s. each.
Women are Strange.
The Hands of Justice.

Robinson (Phil), Works by :
Crown 8vo, cloth extra, 7s. 6d. each.
The Poets' Birds.
The Poets' Beasts.
The Poets and Nature: Reptiles,
Fishes, and Insects. [Preparing.

Rochefoucauld's Maxims and
Moral Reflections. With Notes, and
an Introductory Essay by SAINTE-
BEUVE. Post 8vo, cloth limp, 2s.

Roll of Battle Abbey, The; or,
A List of the Principal Warriors who
came over from Normandy with William the Conqueror, and Settled in
this Country, A.D. 1066-7. With the
principal Arms emblazoned in Gold
and Colours. Handsomely printed, 5s.

Rowley (Hon. Hugh), Works by:
Post 8vo, cloth limp, 2s. 6d. each.
Puniana: Riddles and Jokes. With numerous Illustrations.
More Puniana. Profusely Illustrated.

Runciman (James), Stories by:
Post 8vo, illustrated boards, 2s. each; cloth limp, 2s. 6d. each.
Skippers and Shellbacks.
Grace Balmaign's Sweetheart.
Schools and Scholars.

Russell (W. Clark), Works by:
Crown 8vo, cloth extra, 6s. each; post 8vo, illustrated boards, 2s. each.
Round the Galley-Fire.
On the Fo'k'sle Head.
In the Middle Watch.
A Voyage to the Cape.
Crown 8vo, cloth extra, 6s. each.
A Book for the Hammock.
The Mystery of the "Ocean Star," &c.
₰ The above Six Books may also be had in a handsome cloth box, under the general title of "CLARK RUSSELL'S SEA BOOKS," for 36s.

Sala.—Gaslight and Daylight.
By GEORGE AUGUSTUS SALA. Post 8vo, illustrated boards, 2s.

Sanson.—Seven Generations of Executioners: Memoirs of the Sanson Family (1688 to 1847). Edited by HENRY SANSON. Cr.8vo,cl.ex.3s.6d.

Saunders (John), Novels by:
Crown 8vo, cloth extra, 3s. 6d. each; post 8vo, illustrated boards, 2s. each.
Bound to the Wheel.
Guy Waterman.|Lion in the Path.
The Two Dreamers.
One Against the World. Post 8vo, illustrated boards, 2s.

Saunders (Katharine), Novels by. Cr. 8vo, cloth extra, 3s. 6d. each; post 8vo, illustrated boards, 2s. each.
Margaret and Elizabeth.
The High Mills.
Heart Salvage. | Sebastian.
Joan Merryweather. Post 8vo, illustrated boards, 2s.
Gideon's Rock. Crown 8vo, cloth extra, 3s. 6d.

Science Gossip: An Illustrated Medium of Interchange for Students and Lovers of Nature. Edited by J. E. TAYLOR, F.L.S., &c. Devoted to Geology, Botany, Physiology, Chemistry, Zoology, Microscopy, Telescopy, Physiography, &c. Price 4d. Monthly; or 5s. per year, post free. Vols. I. to XIV. may be had at 7s. 6d. each; and Vols. XV. to date, at 5s. each. Cases for Binding, 1s. 6d. each.

"Secret Out" Series, The:
Cr. 8vo, cl. ex., Illusts., 4s. 6d. each.
The Secret Out: One Thousand Tricks with Cards, and other Recreations; with Entertaining Experiments in Drawing-room or "White Magic." By W. H.CREMER. 300Illusts.
The Art of Amusing: A Collection of Graceful Arts,Games,Tricks,Puzzles, and Charades By FRANK BELLEW. With 300 Illustrations.
Hanky-Panky: Very Easy Tricks, Very Difficult Tricks, White Magic, Sleight of Hand. Edited by W. H. CREMER. With 200 Illustrations.
Magician's Own Book: Performances with Cups and Balls, Eggs, Hats, Handkerchiefs, &c. All from actual Experience. Edited by W. H. CREMER. 200 Illustrations.

Seguin (L. G.), Works by:
Crown 8vo, cloth extra, 6s. each.
The Country of the Passion Play, and the Highlands and Highlanders of Bavaria. With Map and 37 Illusts.
Walks in Algiers and its Surroundings. With 2 Maps and 16 Illusts.

Senior.—By Stream and Sea.
By W.SENIOR. Post 8vo,cl.limp, 2s.6d.

Seven Sagas (The) of Prehistoric Man. By JAMES H. STODDART, Author of "The Village Life." Crown 8vo, cloth extra, 6s.

Shakespeare:
The First Folio Shakespeare.—MR. WILLIAM SHAKESPEARE'S Comedies, Histories, and Tragedies. Published according to the true Originall Copies. London, Printed by ISAAC IAGGARD and ED. BLOUNT. 1623.—A Reproduction of the extremely rare original, in reduced facsimile, by a photographic process—ensuring the strictest accuracy in every detail. Small 8vo, half-Roxburghe, 7s. 6d.
The Lansdowne Shakespeare. Beautifully printed in red and black, in small but very clear type. With engraved facsimile of DROESHOUT's Portrait. Post 8vo, cloth extra, 7s. 6d.
Shakespeare for Children: Tales from Shakespeare. By CHARLES and MARY LAMB. With numerous Illustrations, coloured and plain, by J. MOYR SMITH. Cr. 4to, cl. gilt, 6s.
The Handbook of Shakespeare Music. Being an Account of 350 Pieces of Music, the compositions ranging from the Elizabethan Age to the Present Time. By ALFRED ROFFE. 4to, half-Roxburghe, 7s.
A Study of Shakespeare. By ALGERNON CHARLES SWINBURNE. Crown 8vo, cloth extra, 8s.

Shelley.—The Complete Works

In Verse and Prose of Percy Bysshe Shelley. Edited, Prefaced and Annotated by RICHARD HERNE SHEPHERD. Five Vols., crown 8vo, cloth boards, 3s. 6d. each.

Poetical Works, in Three Vols.

Vol. I. An Introduction by the Editor; The Posthumous Fragments of Margaret Nicholson; Shelley's Correspondence with Stockdale; The Wandering Jew (the only complete version); Queen Mab, with the Notes; Alastor, and other Poems; Rosalind and Helen; Prometheus Unbound; Adonais, &c.

Vol. II. Laon and Cythna (as originally published, instead of the emasculated "Revolt of Islam"); The Cenci; Julian and Maddalo (from Shelley's manuscript); Swellfoot the Tyrant (from the copy in the Dyce Library at South Kensington); The Witch of Atlas; Epipsychidion; Hellas.

Vol. III. Posthumous Poems, published by Mrs. SHELLEY in 1824 and 1839; The Masque of Anarchy (from Shelley's manuscript); and other Pieces not brought together in the ordinary editions.

Prose Works, in Two Vols.

Vol. I. The Two Romances of Zastrozzi and St. Irvyne; the Dublin and Marlow Pamphlets; A Refutation of Deism; Letters to Leigh Hunt, and some Minor Writings and Fragments.

Vol. II. The Essays; Letters from Abroad; Translations and Fragments, Edited by Mrs. SHELLEY, and first published in 1840, with the addition of some Minor Pieces of great interest and rarity, including one recently discovered by Professor DOWDEN. With a Bibliography of Shelley, and an exhaustive Index of the Prose Works.

** Also a LARGE-PAPER EDITION, to be had in SETS only, at 52s. 6d. for the Five Volumes.

Sheridan:—

Sheridan's Complete Works, with Life and Anecdotes. Including his Dramatic Writings, printed from the Original Editions, his Works in Prose and Poetry, Translations, Speeches, Jokes, Puns, &c. With a Collection of Sheridaniana. Crown 8vo, cloth extra, gilt, with 10 full-page Tinted Illustrations, 7s. 6d.

Sheridan's Comedies: The Rivals, and The School for Scandal. Edited, with an Introduction and Notes to each Play, and a Biographical Sketch of Sheridan, by BRANDER MATTHEWS. With Decorative Vignettes and 10 full-page Illusts. Demy 8vo, half-parchment, 12s. 6d.

Sheridan (General).—Personal

Memoirs of General P. H. Sheridan: The Romantic Career of a Great Soldier, told in his Own Words. With 22 Portraits and other Illustrations, 27 Maps and numerous Facsimiles of Famous Letters. Two Vols. of 500 pages each, demy 8vo, cloth extra, 24s.

Sidney's (Sir Philip) Complete

Poetical Works, including all those in "Arcadia." With Portrait, Memorial-Introduction, Notes, &c., by the Rev. A. B. GROSART, D.D. Three Vols., crown 8vo, cloth boards, 18s.

Signboards: Their History.

With Anecdotes of Famous Taverns and Remarkable Characters. By JACOB LARWOOD and JOHN CAMDEN HOTTEN. Crown 8vo, cloth extra, with 100 Illustrations, 7s. 6d.

Sims (George R.), Works by:

Post 8vo, illustrated boards, 2s. each; cloth limp, 2s. 6d. each.

Rogues and Vagabonds.
The Ring o' Bells.
Mary Jane's Memoirs.
Mary Jane Married.

The Dagonet Reciter. Post 8vo, portrait cover, 1s.; cloth, 1s. 6d. [Shortly.

Sister Dora: A Biography. By

MARGARET LONSDALE. Popular Edition, Revised, with additional Chapter, a New Dedication and Preface, and Four Illustrations. Sq. 8vo, picture cover, 4d.; cloth, 6d.

Sketchley.—A Match in the

Dark. By ARTHUR SKETCHLEY. Post 8vo, illustrated boards, 2s.

Slang Dictionary, The: Ety-

mological, Historical, and Anecdotal. Crown 8vo, cloth extra, gilt, 6s. 6d.

Smith (J. Moyr), Works by:

The Prince of Argolis: A Story of the Old Greek Fairy Time. Small 8vo, cloth extra, with 130 Illusts., 3s. 6d.
Tales of Old Thule. With numerous Illustrations. Cr. 8vo, cloth gilt, 6s.
The Wooing of the Water Witch. With Illustrations. Small 8vo, 6s.

Society in London. By A

FOREIGN RESIDENT. Crown 8vo, 1s.; cloth, 1s. 6d.

Society out of Town. By A

FOREIGN RESIDENT, Author of "Society in London." Crown 8vo, cloth extra, 6s. [Preparing.

Society in Paris: The Upper

Ten Thousand. By Count PAUL VASILI. Trans. by RAPHAEL LEDOS DE BEAUFORT. Cr. 8vo, cl. ex., 6s. [Preparing.

Spalding.—Elizabethan Demon-

ology: An Essay in Illustration of the Belief in the Existence of Devils, and the Powers possessed by Them. By T. A. SPALDING, LL.B. Cr. 8vo, cl. ex., 6s.

Speight (T. W.), Novels by:
The Mysteries of Heron Dyke. With a Frontispiece by M. ELLEN EDWARDS. Crown 8vo, cloth extra, 3s. 6d.; post 8vo, illustrated bds., 2s.
Wife or No Wife? Cr. 8vo, picture cover, 1s.; cloth, 1s. 6d.
The Golden Hoop. Post 8vo, illust. boards, 2s.
By Devious Ways. Demy 8vo, 1s. [Nov.

Spenser for Children. By M. H. TOWRY. With Illustrations by WALTER J. MORGAN. Crown 4to, with Coloured Illustrations, cloth gilt, 6s.

Staunton.—Laws and Practice of Chess; Together with an Analysis of the Openings, and a Treatise on End Games. By HOWARD STAUNTON. Edited by ROBERT B. WORMALD. New Edition, small cr. 8vo, cloth extra, 5s.

Stedman (E. C.), Works by:
Victorian Poets. Thirteenth Edition, revised and enlarged. Crown 8vo, cloth extra, 9s.
The Poets of America. Crown 8vo, cloth extra, 9s.

Sterndale.—The Afghan Knife: A Novel. By ROBERT ARMITAGE STERN-DALE. Cr. 8vo, cloth extra, 3s. 6d.; post 8vo, illustrated boards, 2s.

Stevenson (R. Louis), Works by:
Travels with a Donkey in the Cevennes. Sixth Ed. Frontispiece by W. CRANE. Post 8vo, cl. limp, 2s. 6d.
An Inland Voyage. With Front. by W. CRANE. Post 8vo, cl. lp., 2s. 6d.
Familiar Studies of Men and Books. 2nd Edit. Cr. 8vo, buckram extra, 6s.
New Arabian Nights. Crown 8vo, buckram extra, 6s.; post 8vo, illust. boards, 2s.
The Silverado Squatters. With Frontispiece. Crown 8vo, buckram extra, 6s. Cheap Edition, post 8vo, picture cover, 1s.; cloth, 1s. 6d.
Prince Otto: A Romance. Fourth Edition. Crown 8vo, buckram extra, 6s.; post 8vo, illustrated boards, 2s.
The Merry Men, and other Tales and Fables. Cr. 8vo, buckram ex., 6s.
Underwoods: Poems. Post 8vo, cl. ex. 6s.
Memories and Portraits. Second Edition. Cr. 8vo, buckram extra, 6s.
Virginibus Puerisque, and other Papers. A New Edition, Revised. Fcap. 8vo, buckram extra, 6s.

St. John.—A Levantine Family. By BAYLE ST. JOHN. Post 8vo, illus-trated boards, 2s.

Stoddard.—Summer Cruising in the South Seas. By CHARLES WARREN STODDARD. Illust. by WALLIS MACKAY. Crown 8vo, cl. extra, 3s. 6d.

Stories from Foreign Novel-ists. With Notices of their Lives and Writings. By HELEN and ALICE ZIM-MERN. Frontispiece. Crown 8vo, cloth extra, 3s. 6d.; post 8vo, illust. bds., 2s.

St. Pierre.—Paul and Virginia, and The Indian Cottage. By BER-NARDIN ST. PIERRE. Edited, with Life, by Rev. E. CLARKE. Post 8vo, cl. lp., 2s.

Strange Manuscript (A) found in a Copper Cylinder. With 19 full-page Illustrations by GILBERT GAUL. Second Edition. Cr. 8vo, cl. extra, 5s.

Strutt's Sports and Pastimes of the People of England; including the Rural and Domestic Recreations, May Games, Mummeries, Shows, &c., from the Earliest Period to the Present Time. With 140 Illustrations. Edited by WM. HONE. Cr. 8vo, cl. extra, 7s. 6d.

Suburban Homes (The) of London: A Residential Guide to Favourite London Localities, their Society, Celebrities, and Associations. With Notes on their Rental, Rates, and House Accommodation. With Map of Suburban London. Cr. 8vo, cl. ex., 7s 6d.

Swift's Choice Works, in Prose and Verse. With Memoir, Portrait, and Facsimiles of the Maps in the Original Edition of "Gulliver's Travels." Cr. 8vo, cloth extra, 7s. 6d.

Swinburne (Algernon C.), Works by:
Selections from the Poetical Works of Algernon Charles Swinburne. Fcap. 8vo, cloth extra, 6s.
Atalanta in Calydon. Crown 8vo, 6s.
Chastelard. A Tragedy. Cr. 8vo, 7s.
Poems and Ballads. FIRST SERIES. Fcap. 8vo, 9s. Cr. 8vo, same price.
Poems and Ballads. SECOND SERIES. Fcap. 8vo, 9s. Cr. 8vo, same price.
Notes on Poems and Reviews. 8vo, 1s.
Songs before Sunrise. Cr. 8vo, 10s. 6d.
Bothwell: A Tragedy. Cr. 8vo, 12s. 6d.
Songs of Two Nations. Cr. 8vo, 6s.
Essays and Studies. Crown 8vo, 12s.
Erechtheus: A Tragedy. Cr. 8vo, 6s.
Note on Charlotte Bronte. Cr. 8vo, 6s.
A Study of Shakespeare. Cr. 8vo, 8s.
Songs of the Springtides. Cr. 8vo, 6s.
Studies in Song. Crown 8vo, 7s.
Mary Stuart: A Tragedy. Cr. 8vo, 8s.
Tristram of Lyonesse, and other Poems. Crown 8vo, 9s.
A Century of Roundels. Small 4to, 8s.
A Midsummer Holiday, and other Poems. Crown 8vo, 7s.
Marino Faliero: A Tragedy. Cr. 8vo, 6s.
A Study of Victor Hugo. Cr. 8vo, 6s.
Miscellanies. Crown 8vo, 12s.
Locrine: A Tragedy. Crown 8vo, 6s.
Mr. Swinburne's New Volume of Poems. Crown 8vo, 6s. [Shortly.

Symonds.—Wine, Women, and Song: Mediæval Latin Students' Songs. Now first translated into English Verse, with Essay by J. Addington Symonds. Small 8vo, parchment, 6s.

Syntax's (Dr.) Three Tours: In Search of the Picturesque, in Search of Consolation, and in Search of a Wife. With the whole of Rowlandson's droll page Illustrations in Colours and a Life of the Author by J. C. Hotten. Med. 8vo, cloth extra, 7s. 6d.

Taine's History of English Literature. Translated by Henry Van Laun. Four Vols., small 8vo, cloth boards, 30s.—Popular Edition, Two Vols., crown 8vo, cloth extra, 15s.

Taylor's (Bayard) Diversions of the Echo Club: Burlesques of Modern Writers. Post 8vo, cl. limp, 2s.

Taylor (Dr. J. E., F.L.S.), Works by. Crown 8vo, cloth ex., 7s. 6d. each.
The Sagacity and Morality of Plants: A Sketch of the Life and Conduct of the Vegetable Kingdom. Coloured Frontispiece and 100 Illust.
Our Common British Fossils, and Where to Find Them: A Handbook for Students. With 331 Illustrations.
The Playtime Naturalist: A Book for every Home. With about 350 Illustrations. Crown 8vo, cloth extra, 5s. [*Preparing.*]

Taylor's (Tom) Historical Dramas: "Clancarty," "Jeanne Darc," "Twixt Axe and Crown," "The Fool's Revenge," "Arkwright's Wife," "Anne Boleyn," "Plot and Passion." One Vol., cr. 8vo, cloth extra, 7s. 6d.
*** The Plays may also be had separately, at 1s. each.

Tennyson (Lord): A Biographical Sketch. By H. J. Jennings. With a Photograph-Portrait. Crown 8vo, cloth extra, 6s.

Thackerayana: Notes and Anecdotes. Illustrated by Hundreds of Sketches by William Makepeace Thackeray, depicting Humorous Incidents in his School-life, and Favourite Characters in the books of his every-day reading. With Coloured Frontispiece. Cr. 8vo, cl. extra, 7s. 6d.

Thomas (Bertha), Novels by: Crown 8vo, cloth extra, 3s. 6d each; post 8vo, illustrated boards, 2s. each.
Cresslda. | Proud Maisie.
The Violin-Player.

Thomas (M.).—A Fight for Life: A Novel. By W. Moy Thomas. Post 8vo, illustrated boards, 2s.

Thomson's Seasons and Castle of Indolence. With a Biographical and Critical Introduction by Allan Cunningham, and over 50 fine Illustrations on Steel and Wood. Crown 8vo, cloth extra, gilt edges, 7s. 6d.

Thornbury (Walter), Works by Haunted London. Edited by Edward Walford, M.A. With Illustrations by F. W. Fairholt, F.S.A. Crown 8vo, cloth extra, 7s. 6d.
The Life and Correspondence of J. M. W. Turner. Founded upon Letters and Papers furnished by his Friends and fellow Academicians. With numerous Illusts. in Colours, facsimiled from Turner's Original Drawings. Cr. 8vo, cl. extra, 7s. 6d.
Old Stories Re-told. Post 8vo, cloth limp, 2s. 6d.
Tales for the Marines. Post 8vo, illustrated boards, 2s.

Timbs (John), Works by: Crown 8vo, cloth extra, 7s. 6d. each.
The History of Clubs and Club Life in London. With Anecdotes of its Famous Coffee-houses, Hostelries, and Taverns. With many Illusts.
English Eccentrics and Eccentricities: Stories of Wealth and Fashion, Delusions, Impostures, and Fanatic Missions, Strange Sights and Sporting Scenes, Eccentric Artists, Theatrical Folk, Men of Letters, &c. With nearly 50 Illusts.

Trollope (Anthony), Novels by: Crown 8vo, cloth extra, 3s. 6d. each; post 8vo, illustrated boards, 2s. each.
The Way We Live Now.
Kept in the Dark.
Frau Frohmann. | Marion Fay.
Mr. Scarborough's Family.
The Land-Leaguers.
Post 8vo, illustrated boards, 2s. each.
The Golden Lion of Granpere.
John Caldigate. | American Senator

Trollope (Frances E.), Novels by: Crown 8vo, cloth extra, 3s. 6d. each; post 8vo, illustrated boards, 2s. each.
Like Ships upon the Sea.
Mabel's Progress. | Anne Furness.

Trollope (T. A.).—Diamond Cut Diamond, and other Stories. By T. Adolphus Trollope. Post 8vo, illustrated boards, 2s.

Trowbridge.—Farnell's Folly: A Novel. By J. T. Trowbridge. Post 8vo, illustrated boards, 2s.

Turgenieff. — Stories from Foreign Novelists. By Ivan Turgenieff, and others. Cr. 8vo, cloth extra, 3s. 6d.; post 8vo, illustrated boards, 2s.

WANDERER'S LIBRARY, THE, *continued—*
The Story of the London Parks. By JACOB LARWOOD. With Illusts.
London Characters. By HENRY MAYHEW. Illustrated.
Seven Generations of Executioners: Memoirs of the Sanson Family (1688 to 1847). Edited by HENRY SANSON.
Summer Cruising in the South Seas. By C. WARREN STODDARD. Illustrated by WALLIS MACKAY.

Warner.—A Roundabout Journey. By CHARLES DUDLEY WARNER, Author of "My Summer in a Garden." Crown 8vo, cloth extra, 6s.

Warrants, &c. :—
Warrant to Execute Charles I. An exact Facsimile, with the Fifty-nine Signatures, and corresponding Seals. Carefully printed on paper to imitate the Original, 22 in. by 14 in. Price 2s.
Warrant to Execute Mary Queen of Scots. An exact Facsimile, including the Signature of Queen Elizabeth, and a Facsimile of the Great Seal. Beautifully printed on paper to imitate the Original MS. Price 2s.
Magna Charta. An exact Facsimile of the Original Document in the British Museum, printed on fine plate paper, nearly 3 feet long by 2 feet wide, with the Arms and Seals emblazoned in Gold and Colours. 5s.
The Roll of Battle Abbey; or, A List of the Principal Warriors who came over from Normandy with William the Conqueror, and Settled in this Country, A.D. 1066-7. With the principal Arms emblazoned in Gold and Colours. Price 5s.

Wayfarer, The : Journal of the Society of Cyclists. Published at short intervals. Price 1s. The Numbers for OCTOBER, 1886, JANUARY, MAY, and OCTOBER, 1887, and FEBRUARY, 1888, are now ready.

Weather, How to Foretell the, with the Pocket Spectroscope. By F. W. CORY, M.R.C.S. Eng., F.R.Met. Soc., &c. With 10 Illustrations. Crown 8vo, 1s. ; cloth, 1s. 6d.

Westropp.—Handbook of Pottery and Porcelain; or, History of those Arts from the Earliest Period. By HODDER M. WESTROPP. With numerous Illustrations, and a List of Marks. Crown 8vo, cloth limp, 4s. 6d.

Whist. — How to Play Solo Whist: Its Method and Principles Explained, and its Practice Demonstrated. With Illustrative Specimen Hands in red and black, and a Revised and Augmented Code of Laws. By ABRAHAM S. WILKS and CHARLES F. PARDON. Crown 8vo, cloth extra, 3s. 6d.

Whistler's (Mr.) "Ten o'Clock." Uniform with his " Whistler v. Ruskin: Art and Art Critics." Cr. 8vo, 1s.

Williams (W. Mattieu, F.R.A.S.), Works by :
Science Notes. See the GENTLEMAN'S MAGAZINE. 1s. Monthly.
Science in Short Chapters. Crown 8vo, cloth extra, 7s. 6d.
A Simple Treatise on Heat. Crown 8vo, cloth limp, with Illusts., 2s. 6d.
The Chemistry of Cookery. Crown 8vo, cloth extra, 6s.

Wilson (Dr. Andrew, F.R.S.E.), Works by :
Chapters on Evolution: A Popular History of Darwinian and Allied Theories of Development. 3rd ed. Cr. 8vo, cl. ex., with 259 Illusts., 7s. 6d.
Leaves from a Naturalist's Notebook. Post 8vo, cloth limp, 2s. 6d.
Leisure-Time Studies, chiefly Biological. Third Edit., with New Preface. Cr. 8vo, cl. ex., with Illusts., 6s.
Studies in Life and Sense. With numerous Illusts. Cr. 8vo, cl. ex., 6s.
Common Accidents, and How to Treat them. By Dr. ANDREW WILSON and others. With numerous Illusts. Cr. 8vo, 1s. ; cl. limp, 1s. 6d.

Winter (J. S.), Stories by :
Post 8vo, illustrated boards, 2s. each.
Cavalry Life.
Regimental Legends.

Women of the Day : A Biographical Dictionary of Notable Contemporaries. By FRANCES HAYS. Crown 8vo, cloth extra, 5s.

Wood.—Sabina: A Novel. By Lady WOOD. Post 8vo, illust. bds., 2s.

Wood (H. F.)—The Passenger from Scotland Yard: A Detective Story. By H. F. WOOD. Crown 8vo, cloth extra, 6s.; post 8vo, illust. bds.,2s.

Words, Facts, and Phrases : A Dictionary of Curious, Quaint, and Out-of-the-Way Matters. By ELIEZER EDWARDS. New and cheaper issue, cr. 8vo, cl. ex., 7s. 6d. ; half-bound, 9s.

Wright (Thomas), Works by :
Crown 8vo, cloth extra, 7s. 6d. each.
Caricature History of the Georges. (The House of Hanover.) With 400 Pictures, Caricatures, Squibs, Broadsides, Window Pictures, &c.
History of Caricature and of the Grotesque in Art, Literature, Sculpture, and Painting. Profusely Illustrated by F.W. FAIRHOLT, F.S.A.

Yates (Edmund), Novels by :
Post 8vo, illustrated boards, 2s. each.
Castaway. | The Forlorn Hope.
Land at Last.

NEW NOVELS.

A Strange Manuscript found in a Copper Cylinder. Illustrated by GIL-BERT GAUL. Cr. 8vo, 5s.

The Legacy of Cain. By WILKIE COLLINS. 3 Vols., cr. 8vo. [*Shortly.*

For Faith and Freedom. By WALTER BESANT. 3 Vols., cr. 8vo. [*Shortly.*

This Mortal Coil. By GRANT ALLEN. 3 Vols., crown 8vo.

The Blackhall Ghosts. By SARAH TYTLER. 3 Vols., cr. 8vo. [*Shortly.*

Agatha Page. By ISAAC HENDERSON. 2 Vols., crown 8vo. [*Shortly.*

THE PICCADILLY NOVELS.

Popular Stories by the Best Authors. LIBRARY EDITIONS, many Illustrated, crown 8vo, cloth extra, 3s. 6d. each.

BY GRANT ALLEN.
Philistia.
For Maimie's Sake.
The Devil's Die.

BY THE AUTHOR OF "JOHN HERRING."
Red Spider. | Eve.

BY W. BESANT & JAMES RICE.
Ready-Money Mortiboy.
My Little Girl.
The Case of Mr. Lucraft.
This Son of Vulcan.
With Harp and Crown.
The Golden Butterfly.
By Celia's Arbour.
The Monks of Thelema.
'Twas in Trafalgar's Bay.
The Seamy Side.
The Ten Years' Tenant.
The Chaplain of the Fleet.

BY WALTER BESANT.
All Sorts and Conditions of Men.
The Captains' Room.
All in a Garden Fair.
Dorothy Forster. | Uncle Jack.
Children of Gibeon.
The World Went Very Well Then.

BY ROBERT BUCHANAN.
Child of Nature.
God and the Man.
The Shadow of the Sword.
The Martyrdom of Madeline.
Love Me for Ever.
Annan Water. | The New Abelard.
Matt. | Foxglove Manor.
The Master of the Mine.
The Heir of Linne.

BY HALL CAINE.
The Shadow of a Crime.
A Son of Hagar. | The Deemster.

BY MRS. H. LOVETT CAMERON.
Deceivers Ever. | Juliet's Guardian.

BY MORTIMER COLLINS.
Sweet Anne Page. | Transmigration.
From Midnight to Midnight.

MORTIMER & FRANCES COLLINS.
Blacksmith and Scholar.
The Village Comedy.
You Play me False.

BY WILKIE COLLINS.
Antonina.
Basil.
Hide and Seek.
The Dead Secret.
Queen of Hearts.
My Miscellanies.
Woman in White.
The Moonstone.
Man and Wife.
Poor Miss Finch.
Miss or Mrs.?
New Magdalen.
The Frozen Deep.
The Law and the Lady.
The Two Destinies
Haunted Hotel.
The Fallen Leaves
Jezebel's Daughter
The Black Robe.
Heart and Science
"I Say No."
Little Novels.
The Evil Genius.

BY DUTTON COOK.
Paul Foster's Daughter.

BY WILLIAM CYPLES.
Hearts of Gold.

BY ALPHONSE DAUDET.
The Evangelist; or, Port Salvation.

BY JAMES DE MILLE.
A Castle in Spain.

BY J. LEITH DERWENT.
Our Lady of Tears.
Circe's Lovers.

BY M. BETHAM-EDWARDS.
Felicia.

BY MRS. ANNIE EDWARDES.
Archie Lovell.

BY PERCY FITZGERALD.
Fatal Zero.

BY R. E. FRANCILLON.
Queen Cophetua.
One by One.
A Real Queen.
King or Knave?
Prefaced by Sir BARTLE FRERE.
Pandurang Hari.

BY EDWARD GARRETT.
The Capel Girls.

PICCADILLY NOVELS, *continued*—
BY CHARLES GIBBON.
Robin Gray.
What will the World Say?
In Honour Bound.
Queen of the Meadow.
The Flower of the Forest.
A Heart's Problem.
The Braes of Yarrow.
The Golden Shaft.
Of High Degree.
Loving a Dream.

BY THOMAS HARDY.
Under the Greenwood Tree.

BY JULIAN HAWTHORNE.
Garth.
Ellice Quentin.
Sebastian Strome.
Dust.
Fortune's Fool.
Beatrix Randolph.
David Poindexter's Disappearance.

BY SIR A. HELPS.
Ivan de Biron.

BY MRS. ALFRED HUNT
Thornicroft's Model.
The Leaden Casket.
Self-Condemned.
That other Person.

BY JEAN INGELOW.
Fated to be Free.

BY R. ASHE KING.
A Drawn Game.
"The Wearing of the Green."

BY HENRY KINGSLEY.
Number Seventeen.

BY E. LYNN LINTON.
Patricia Kemball.
Atonement of Leam Dundas.
The World Well Lost.
Under which Lord?
"My Love!"
Ione.
Paston Carew.

BY HENRY W. LUCY.
Gideon Fleyce.

BY JUSTIN McCARTHY.
The Waterdale Neighbours.
A Fair Saxon.
Dear Lady Disdain.
Miss Misanthrope.
Donna Quixote.
The Comet of a Season.
Maid of Athens.
Camiola.

BY MRS. MACDONELL.
Quaker Cousins.

BY FLORENCE MARRYAT.
Open! Sesame! | Written in Fire.

PICCADILLY NOVELS, *continued*—
BY D. CHRISTIE MURRAY.
Life's Atonement. | Coals of Fire.
Joseph's Coat. | Val Strange.
A Model Father. | Hearts.
By the Gate of the Sea.
The Way of the World.
A Bit of Human Nature.
First Person Singular.
Cynic Fortune.

BY MRS. OLIPHANT.
Whiteladies.

BY OUIDA.
Held in Bondage. | Two Little Wooden
Strathmore. | Shoes.
Chandos. | In a Winter City.
Under Two Flags. | Ariadne.
Idalia. | Friendship.
Cecil Castle- | Moths.
maine's Gage. | Pipistrello.
Tricotrin. | A Village Com-
Puck. | mune.
Folle Farine. | Bimbi.
A Dog of Flanders. | Wanda.
Pascarel. | Frescoes.
Signa. [ine. | In Maremma.
Princess Naprax- | Othmar.

BY MARGARET A. PAUL.
Gentle and Simple.

BY JAMES PAYN.
Lost Sir Massing- | From Exile.
berd. | A Grape from a
Walter's Word. | Thorn.
Less Black than | Some Private
We're Painted. | Views.
By Proxy. | The Canon's
High Spirits. | Ward.
Under One Roof. | Talk of the Town.
A Confidential | Glow-worm Tales.
Agent.

BY E. C. PRICE.
Valentina. | The Foreigners.
Mrs. Lancaster's Rival.

BY CHARLES READE.
It is Never Too Late to Mend.
Hard Cash. | Peg Woffington.
Christie Johnstone.
Griffith Gaunt. | Foul Play.
The Double Marriage.
Love Me Little, Love Me Long.
The Cloister and the Hearth.
The Course of True Love.
The Autobiography of a Thief.
Put Yourself in His Place.
A Terrible Temptation.
The Wandering Heir. | A Simpleton.
A Woman-Hater. | Readiana.
Singleheart and Doubleface.
The Jilt.
Good Stories of Men and other
Animals.

BY MRS. J. H. RIDDELL.
Her Mother's Darling.
Prince of Wales's Garden-Party.
Weird Stories.

Tytler (C. C. Fraser-). — Mistress Judith: A Novel. By C. C. FRASER-TYTLER. Cr. 8vo, cloth extra, 3s. 6d.; post 8vo, illust. boards, 2s.

Tytler (Sarah), Novels by:
Crown 8vo, cloth extra, 3s. 6d. each; post 8vo, illustrated boards, 2s. each.
What She Came Through.
The Bride's Pass.
Saint Mungo's City.
Beauty and the Beast.
Noblesse Oblige.
Lady Bell.
Citoyenne Jacqueline.

Crown 8vo, cloth extra, 3s. 6d. each.
The Huguenot Family. With Illusts.
Buried Diamonds.

Disappeared: A Romance. Post 8vo, illustrated boards, 2s.
The Blackhall Ghosts: A Novel. 3 Vols., crown 8vo. [*Preparing.*

Van Laun.—History of French Literature. By H. VAN LAUN. Three Vols., demy 8vo, cl. bds., 7s. 6d. each.

Villari.— A Double Bond: A Story. By LINDA VILLARI. Fcap. 8vo, picture cover, 1s.

Walford (Edw., M.A.), Works by:
The County Families of the United Kingdom. Containing Notices of the Descent, Birth, Marriage, Education, &c., of more than 12000, distinguished Heads of Families, their Heirs Apparent or Presumptive, the Offices they hold or have held, their Town and Country Addresses, Clubs, &c. Twenty-seventh Annual Edition, for 1888, cloth gilt, 50s.
The Shilling Peerage (1888). Containing an Alphabetical List of the House of Lords, Dates of Creation, Lists of Scotch and Irish Peers, Addresses, &c. 32mo, cloth, 1s.
The Shilling Baronetage (1888). Containing an Alphabetical List of the Baronets of the United Kingdom, short Biographical Notices, Dates of Creation, Addresses, &c. 32mo, cloth, 1s.
The Shilling Knightage (1888). Containing an Alphabetical List of the Knights of the United Kingdom, short Biographical Notices. Dates of Creation, Addresses,&c. 32mo,cl.,1s.
The Shilling House of Commons (1888). Containing a List of all the Members of Parliament, their Town and Country Addresses, &c. New Edition, embodying the results of the recent General Election. 32mo, cloth, 1s.

Walford's (Edw.) Works, *continued—*
The Complete Peerage, Baronetage, Knightage, and House of Commons (1888). In One Volume, royal 32mo, cloth extra, gilt edges, 5s.
Haunted London. By WALTER THORNBURY. Edited by EDWARD WALFORD, M.A. With Illustrations by F. W. FAIRHOLT, F.S.A. Crown 8vo, cloth extra, 7s. 6d.

Walton and Cotton's Complete Angler; or, The Contemplative Man's Recreation; being a Discourse of Rivers, Fishponds, Fish and Fishing, written by IZAAK WALTON; and Instructions how to Angle for a Trout or Grayling in a clear Stream, by CHARLES COTTON. With Original Memoirs and Notes by Sir HARRIS NICOLAS, and 61 Copperplate Illustrations. Large crown 8vo, cloth antique, 7s. 6d.

Walt Whitman, Poems by. Selected and edited, with an Introduction, by WILLIAM M. ROSSETTI. A New Edition, with a Steel Plate Portrait. Crown 8vo, printed on handmade paper and bound in buckram, 6s.

Wanderer's Library, The:
Crown 8vo, cloth extra, 3s. 6d. each.
Wanderings in Patagonia; or, Life among the Ostrich-Hunters. By JULIUS BEERBOHM. Illustrated.
Camp Notes: Stories of Sport and Adventure in Asia, Africa, and America. By FREDERICK BOYLE.
Savage Life. By FREDERICK BOYLE.
Merrie England in the Olden Time. By GEORGE DANIEL. With Illustrations by ROBT. CRUIKSHANK.
Circus Life and Circus Celebrities. By THOMAS FROST.
The Lives of the Conjurers. By THOMAS FROST.
The Old Showmen and the Old London Fairs. By THOMAS FROST.
Low-Life Deeps. An Account of the Strange Fish to be found there. By JAMES GREENWOOD.
The Wilds of London. By JAMES GREENWOOD.
Tunis: The Land and the People. By the Chevalier de HESSE-WARTEGG. With 22 Illustrations.
The Life and Adventures of a Cheap Jack. By One of the Fraternity. Edited by CHARLES HINDLEY.
The World Behind the Scenes. By PERCY FITZGERALD.
Tavern Anecdotes and Sayings: Including the Origin of Signs, and Reminiscences connected with Taverns, Coffee Houses, Clubs, &c. By CHARLES HINDLEY. With Illusts.
The Genial Showman: Life and Adventures of Artemus Ward. By E. P. HINGSTON. With a Frontispiece.

CHEAP POPULAR NOVELS, *continued—*
WILKIE COLLINS, *continued.*

Man and Wife.	Haunted Hotel.
Poor Miss Finch.	The Fallen Leaves.
Miss or Mrs.?	Jezebel's Daughter
New Magdalen.	The Black Robe.
The Frozen Deep.	Heart and Science
Law and the Lady.	"I Say No."
The Two Destinies	The Evil Genius.

BY *MORTIMER COLLINS.*

Sweet Anne Page.	From Midnight to
Transmigration.	Midnight.
A Fight with Fortune.	

MORTIMER & FRANCES COLLINS.
Sweet and Twenty. | Frances.
Blacksmith and Scholar.
The Village Comedy.
You Play me False.

BY *M. J. COLQUHOUN.*
Every Inch a Soldier.

BY *MONCURE D. CONWAY.*
Pine and Palm.

BY *DUTTON COOK.*
Leo. | Paul Foster's Daughter.

BY *C. EGBERT CRADDOCK.*
The Prophet of the Great Smoky Mountains.

BY *WILLIAM CYPLES.*
Hearts of Gold.

BY *ALPHONSE DAUDET.*
The Evangelist; or, Port Salvation.

BY *JAMES DE MILLE.*
A Castle in Spain.

BY *J. LEITH DERWENT.*
Our Lady of Tears. | Circe's Lovers.

BY *CHARLES DICKENS.*
Sketches by Boz. | Oliver Twist.
Pickwick Papers. | Nicholas Nickleby

BY *DICK DONOVAN.*
The Man-Hunter.

BY *MRS. ANNIE EDWARDES.*
A Point of Honour. | Archie Lovell.

BY *M. BETHAM-EDWARDS.*
Felicia. | Kitty.

BY *EDWARD EGGLESTON.*
Roxy.

BY *PERCY FITZGERALD.*
Bella Donna. | Never Forgotten.
The Second Mrs. Tillotson.
Polly. | Fatal Zero.
Seventy-five Brooke Street.
The Lady of Brantome.

BY *ALBANY DE FONBLANQUE.*
Filthy Lucre.

BY *R. E. FRANCILLON.*
Olympia. | Queen Cophetua.
One by One. | A Real Queen.

BY *HAROLD FREDERIC.*
Seth's Brother's Wife.

Prefaced by Sir H. BARTLE FRERE.
Pandurang Hari.

BY *HAIN FRISWELL.*
One of Two.

BY *EDWARD GARRETT.*
The Capel Girls.

CHEAP POPULAR NOVELS, *continued—*
BY *CHARLES GIBBON.*

Robin Gray.	The Flower of the
For Lack of Gold.	Forest.
What will the	Braes of Yarrow.
World Say?	The Golden Shaft.
In Honour Bound.	Of High Degree.
In Love and War.	Fancy Free.
For the King.	Mead and Stream.
In Pastures Green	Loving a Dream.
Queen of the Mea-	A Hard Knot.
dow.	Heart's Delight.
A Heart's Problem	

BY *WILLIAM GILBERT.*
Dr. Austin's Guests. | James Duke.
The Wizard of the Mountain.

BY *JAMES GREENWOOD.*
Dick Temple.

BY *JOHN HABBERTON.*
Brueton's Bayou. | Country Luck.

BY *ANDREW HALLIDAY*
Every-Day Papers.

BY *LADY DUFFUS HARDY.*
Paul Wynter's Sacrifice.

BY *THOMAS HARDY.*
Under the Greenwood Tree.

BY *J. BERWICK HARWOOD.*
The Tenth Earl.

BY *JULIAN HAWTHORNE.*

Garth.	Sebastian Strome
Ellice Quentin.	Dust.
Prince Saroni's Wife.	
Fortune's Fool.	Beatrix Randolph.
Miss Cadogna.	Love—or a Name.

BY *SIR ARTHUR HELPS.*
Ivan de Biron.

BY *MRS. CASHEL HOEY.*
The Lover's Creed.

BY *TOM HOOD.*
A Golden Heart.

BY *MRS. GEORGE HOOPER.*
The House of Raby.

BY *TIGHE HOPKINS.*
'Twixt Love and Duty.

BY *MRS. ALFRED HUNT.*
Thornicroft's Model.
The Leaden Casket.
Self-Condemned.
That other Person.

BY *JEAN INGELOW.*
Fated to be Free.

BY *HARRIETT JAY.*
The Dark Colleen.
The Queen of Connaught.

BY *MARK KERSHAW*
Colonial Facts and Fictions.

BY *R. ASHE KING*
A Drawn Game.
"The Wearing of the Green."

BY *HENRY KINGSLEY*
Oakshott Castle.

BY *JOHN LEYS.*
The Lindsays.

BY *MARY LINSKILL.*
In Exchange for a Soul.

BY *E. LYNN LINTON.*
Patricia Kemball.
The Atonement of Leam Dundas.

CHEAP POPULAR NOVELS, *continued—*
E. LYNN LINTON, *continued—*
The World Well Lost.
Under Which Lord ?
With a Silken Thread.
The Rebel of the Family.
"My Love." | Ione.

BY HENRY W. LUCY.
Gideon Fleyce.

BY JUSTIN McCARTHY.
Dear Lady Disdain | Miss Misanthrope
The Waterdale | Donna Quixote.
Neighbours. | The Comet of a
My Enemy's | Season.
Daughter. | Maid of Athens.
A Fair Saxon. | Camiola.
Linley Rochford. |

BY MRS. MACDONELL.
Quaker Cousins.

BY KATHARINE S. MACQUOID.
The Evil Eye. | Lost Rose.

BY W. H. MALLOCK.
The New Republic.

BY FLORENCE MARRYAT.
Open! Sesame. | Fighting the Air.
A Harvest of Wild | Written In Fire.
Oats. |

BY J. MASTERMAN.
Half-a-dozen Daughters.

BY BRANDER MATTHEWS.
A Secret of the Sea.

BY JEAN MIDDLEMASS.
Touch and Go. | Mr. Dorillion.

BY MRS. MOLESWORTH.
Hathercourt Rectory.

BY D. CHRISTIE MURRAY.
A Life's Atonement | Hearts.
A Model Father. | Way of the World.
Joseph's Coat. | A Bit of Human
Coals of Fire. | Nature.
By the Gate of the | First Person Sin-
Sea. | gular.
Val Strange | Cynic Fortune.
Old Blazer's Hero. |

BY ALICE O'HANLON.
The Unforeseen.

BY MRS. OLIPHANT.
Whiteladies. | The Primrose Path.
The Greatest Heiress in England.

BY MRS. ROBERT O'REILLY.
Phœbe's Fortunes.

BY OUIDA.
Held In Bondage. | Two Little Wooden
Strathmore. | Shoes.
Chandos. | In a Winter City.
Under Two Flags. | Ariadne.
Idalia. | Friendship.
Cecil Castle- | Moths.
maine's Gage. | Pipistrello.
Tricotrin. | A Village Com-
Puck. | mune.
Folle Farine. | Bimbi.
A Dog of Flanders. | Wanda.
Pascarel. | Frescoes
Signa. [ine. | In Maremma.
Princess Naprax- | Othmar.

CHEAP POPULAR NOVELS, *continued—*
BY MARGARET AGNES PAUL.
Gentle and Simple.

BY JAMES PAYN.
Lost Sir Massing- | Like Father, Like
berd. | Son.
A Perfect Trea- | Marine Residence.
sure. | Married Beneath
Bentinck's Tutor. | Him.
Murphy's Master. | Mirk Abbey. [Won
A County Family. | Not Wooed, but
At Her Mercy. | Less Black than
A Woman's Ven- | We're Painted.
geance. | By Proxy.
Cecil's Tryst. | Under One Roof.
Clyffards of Clyffe | High Spirits.
The Family Scape- | Carlyon's Year.
grace. | A Confidential
Foster Brothers. | Agent.
Found Dead. | Some Private
Best of Husbands. | Views.
Walter's Word. | From Exile.
Halves. | A Grape from a
Fallen Fortunes. | Thorn.
What He Cost Her | For Cash Only.
Humorous Stories | Kit : A Memory.
Gwendoline's Har- | The Canon's Ward
vest. | Talk of the Town.
£200 Reward. | Holiday Tasks.

BY C. L. PIRKIS.
Lady Lovelace.

BY EDGAR A. POE.
The Mystery of Marie Roget.

BY E. C. PRICE.
Valentina. | The Foreigners
Mrs. Lancaster's Rival.
Gerald.

BY CHARLES READE.
It Is Never Too Late to Mend.
Hard Cash. | Peg Woffington.
Christie Johnstone.
Griffith Gaunt.
Put Yourself In His Place.
The Double Marriage.
Love Me Little, Love Me Long.
Foul Play.
The Cloister and the Hearth.
The Course of True Love.
Autobiography of a Thief.
A Terrible Temptation.
The Wandering Heir.
A Simpleton. | A Woman-Hater.
Readiana. | The Jilt.
Singleheart and Doubleface.
Good Stories of Men and other
Animals.

BY MRS. J. H. RIDDELL.
Her Mother's Darling.
Prince of Wales's Garden Party.
Weird Stories. | Fairy Water.
The Uninhabited House.
The Mystery In Palace Gardens.

BY F. W. ROBINSON.
Women are Strange.
The Hands of Justice.

CHEAP POPULAR NOVELS, *continued*—
BY JAMES RUNCIMAN.
Skippers and Shellbacks.
Grace Balmaign's Sweetheart.
Schools and Scholars.
BY W. CLARK RUSSELL.
Round the Galley Fire.
On the Fo'k'sle Head.
In the Middle Watch.
A Voyage to the Cape.
BY BAYLE ST. JOHN.
A Levantine Family.
BY GEORGE AUGUSTUS SALA.
Gaslight and Daylight.
BY JOHN SAUNDERS.
Bound to the Wheel.
One Against the World.
Guy Waterman. | Two Dreamers.
The Lion in the Path.
BY KATHARINE SAUNDERS.
Joan Merryweather.
Margaret and Elizabeth.
The High Mills.
Heart Salvage. | Sebastian.
BY GEORGE R. SIMS.
Rogues and Vagabonds.
The Ring o' Bells.
Mary Jane's Memoirs.
Mary Jane Married.
BY ARTHUR SKETCHLEY.
A Match in the Dark.
BY T. W. SPEIGHT.
The Mysteries of Heron Dyke.
The Golden Hoop.
BY R. A. STERNDALE.
The Afghan Knife.
BY R. LOUIS STEVENSON.
New Arabian Nights. | Prince Otto.
BY BERTHA THOMAS.
Cressida. | Proud Maisie.
The Violin-Player.
BY W. MOY THOMAS.
A Fight for Life.
BY WALTER THORNBURY.
Tales for the Marines.
BY T. ADOLPHUS TROLLOPE.
Diamond Cut Diamond.
BY ANTHONY TROLLOPE.
The Way We Live Now.
The American Senator.
Frau Frohmann. | Marion Fay.
Kept in the Dark.
Mr. Scarborough's Family.
The Land-Leaguers.
The Golden Lion of Granpere.
John Caldigate.
By F. ELEANOR TROLLOPE.
Like Ships upon the Sea.
Anne Furness. | Mabel's Progress.
BY J. T. TROWBRIDGE.
Farnell's Folly.
BY IVAN TURGENIEFF, &c.
Stories from Foreign Novelists.
BY MARK TWAIN.
Tom Sawyer. | A Tramp Abroad.

CHEAP POPULAR NOVELS, *continued*—
MARK TWAIN, *continued*.
A Pleasure Trip on the Continent
of Europe.
The Stolen White Elephant.
Huckleberry Finn.
Life on the Mississippi.
The Prince and the Pauper.
BY C. C. FRASER-TYTLER.
Mistress Judith.
BY SARAH TYTLER.
What She Came Through.
The Bride's Pass.
Saint Mungo's City.
Beauty and the Beast.
Lady Bell. | Noblesse Oblige.
Citoyenne Jacqueline | Disappeared
BY J. S. WINTER.
Cavalry Life. | Regimental Legends.
BY H. F. WOOD.
The Passenger from Scotland Yard.
BY LADY WOOD.
Sabina.
BY EDMUND YATES.
Castaway. | The Forlorn Hope.
Land at Last.
ANONYMOUS.
Paul Ferroll.
Why Paul Ferroll Killed his Wife.
POPULAR SHILLING BOOKS.
Jeff Briggs's Love Story. By BRET
HARTE.   [BRET HARTE.
The Twins of Table Mountain. By
A Day's Tour. By PERCY FITZGERALD.
Mrs. Gainsborough's Diamonds. By
JULIAN HAWTHORNE.
A Dream and a Forgetting. By ditto.
A Romance of the Queen's Hounds.
By CHARLES JAMES.
Kathleen Mavourneen. By Author
of "That Lass o' Lowrie's."
Lindsay's Luck. By the Author of
"That Lass o' Lowrie's."
Pretty Polly Pemberton. By the
Author of "That Lass o' Lowrie's."
Trooping with Crows. By C. L. PIRKIS
The Professor's Wife. By L. GRAHAM.
A Double Bond. By LINDA VILLARI.
Esther's Glove. By R. E. FRANCILLON.
The Garden that Paid the Rent
By TOM JERROLD.
Curly. By JOHN COLEMAN. Illus-
trated by J. C. DOLLMAN.
Beyond the Gates. By E. S. PHELPS.
Old Maid's Paradise. By E. S. PHELPS.
Burglars in Paradise. By E. S. PHELPS.
Jack the Fisherman. By E. S. PHELPS.
Doom: An Atlantic Episode. By
JUSTIN H. MCCARTHY, M.P.
Our Sensation Novel. Edited by
JUSTIN H MCCARTHY, M.P.
Bible Characters. By CHAS. READE.
The Dagonet Reciter. By G. R. SIMS.
Wife or No Wife? By T. W. SPEIGHT.
By Devious Ways. By T. W. SPEIGHT.
The Silverado Squatters. By R.
LOUIS STEVENSON.

J. OGDEN AND CO. LIMITED, PRINTERS, GREAT SAFFRON HILL, E.C.